HR Transformation Technology

HR Transformation Technology

Delivering Systems to Support the New HR Model

ALLAN BOROUGHS, LES PALMER and IAN HUNTER

GOWER

Published by
Gower Publishing Limited
Gower House
Croft Road
Aldershot
Hampshire GU11 3HR
England

Ashgate Publishing Company
Suite 420
101 Cherry Street
Burlington, VT 05401-4405
USA

Ian Hunter, Les Palmer and Allan Boroughs have asserted their moral right under the Copyright, Designs and Patents Act, 1988, to be identified as the authors of this work.

British Library Cataloguing in Publication Data
Hunter, Ian, 1963–
    HR transformation technology : delivering systems to support the new HR model
    1. Personnel management – Data processing
    I. Title II. Palmer, Les III. Boroughs, Allan
    658.3'00285

    ISBN-13: 9780566088339

Library of Congress Cataloging-in-Publication Data
Hunter, Ian, 1963–
    HR transformation technology : delivering systems to support the new HR model / by Ian Hunter, Les Palmer, and Allan Boroughs.
        p. cm.
    Includes index.
    ISBN 978-0-566-08833-9
    1. Personnel management--Technological innovations. 2. Management information systems. 3. Personnel management--Data processing. I. Palmer, Les. II. Boroughs, Allan. III. Title.

    HF5549.5.T33H86 2008
    658.300285--dc22

                                                                                    2007039714

Printed and bound in Great Britain by TJ International Ltd, Padstow, Cornwall.

Contents

List of Figures

List of Tables

Acknowledgements

We would like to acknowledge and thank the following people: Jean Timms (Norwich Union), Neil Pearse (Fujitsu Telecommunications Europe), Bernard O'Driscoll (Lloyds TSB), Jim O'Connell (NHS), Martin Hunt and Bobby Whitelock.

Ian and Allan would also like to extend their thanks to Emma Hunter and to Carol Boroughs for their help in researching and preparing this book.

PART I

The Role of Technology in the HR Function

How the HR Function has Evolved

The Complexity of the IT Challenge

The development of human resources is bound inextricably to the technology that serves it. The HR function has faced a succession of demands for changes to the way in which it delivers transactional services ranging from the development of more effective, integrated end-to-end processes through to the development of knowledge-based centres of excellence.

In the end, however, the ability of the HR function to deliver step changes in performance is dependent on its capability to manage administrative tasks, which in turn demands a firm grasp and control of HR processes and data.

The exasperated phrase 'we can't produce a simple headcount figure' has frequently been heard in many organizations unable to get to grips with the complexity of fast-moving HR information, even after they may have invested considerable sums of money in systems to try to raise the capabilities of the HR function.

The clue to the problem lies in the phrase itself: an employee headcount is rarely a 'simple figure'. For example, producing an accurate headcount often demands a clear definition of parameters:

- Does the figure include staff on maternity leave or career breaks?

- Does it count individual people or full-time equivalents (FTEs)?

- Does it include contractors, temporary and agency staff (regardless of how much of a permanent fixture they may be)?

- Given the fact that resourcing is a highly dynamic process, what day of the month is this figure taken from?

Once these questions are considered, it becomes apparent that seemingly simple data such as headcount in fact define a process for tracking an employee population.

Further complications may arise when the headcount data are compared to similar figures produced by other systems. How often have HR staff wrestled to reconcile their headcount figures with those of payroll or pensions, who may be using subtle variations on the parameters selected by HR? Similarly, finance operations may confound the issue further by carving the organization differently from HR. Clearly when cost centres don't line up in an obvious way with organization structures, then aligning headcount with staff costs becomes a nightmarish task. Small wonder that many organizations have wondered aloud where the promised efficiency savings were coming from.

The situation is no simpler around the management of integrated HR processes. For example, the benefits of an integrated HR and payroll operation, whilst well documented, are still frequently unrealised. A lack of integration around legacy systems frequently shows up in HR as separate HR and payroll systems.

Consequently the organization and delivery of HR and payroll services is defined not by what works best for the customer/employee, but by where the boundaries of the software lie.

Interfaces between systems too often define the divisions between departments, for example where HR data on employee movements are passed clumsily across to payroll, causing the process to stutter and requiring manual intervention, recalculation and double entry of data.

Such data and process management problems and resultant inferior service quality have been a recurring historical problem in HR that has, arguably, been a contributing factor in the inability of the function to participate fully in the strategic agenda.

Against this background of struggling to make technology deliver, HR is now facing a new challenge in terms of the way its services are organized and delivered. The separation of administrative/operational activity into shared service centres, together with the development of the role of the HR business partner to deliver strategic advice and support directly to the business, have set new standards of process and data management for HR to achieve.

However, there is unlikely to be much tolerance for HR failing to deliver benefits from the new HR model and blaming the historic problems on poor technology. Many organizations are pushing the operational effectiveness agenda hard, motivated by clear success stories around shared services in different organizations. In some sectors, such as government, the objectives have been formalized – for example, as in the Gershon report, demanding fixed levels of operational improvement in a given timescale.

The move to more effective HR operations and technology is not simply aspirational; it is a clear demand from the business. This demand is given added edge as, for many organizations, the development of HR shared services is simply one option, with the other being to source such services from commercial external providers.

In our own experience, we have seen an increasing number of organizations approach the transformation of HR operations with an open mind as to whether the solution should be 'built' or 'bought'. The implications for HR are clear: delivery of HR services needs to make a step change in performance to keep pace with demand from regulators and shareholders, or be considered a prime target for outsourcing. Against this background, reliance on legacy technologies with their inherent problems and high cost is simply not going to cut it!

In this book we will explore the HR technology architectures that underpin the new HR model and illustrate how organizations can best leverage technology to serve the process of HR change.

We will look at the implications of the new HR model in terms of new users' roles and their needs. We will see how the HR infrastructure has evolved to accommodate the needs of HR business partners, centres of excellence and HR shared service centres and we will follow the process for defining and delivering a working architecture, appropriately scaled to the organization that supports the HR transformation process.

Development of the Traditional HR Model

For most organizations there was little significant development of the HR or as, it was then more commonly known, the 'Personnel' function prior to the 1960s, and the focus sat mainly with the administration of core activities such as payroll or timesheets.

Rapid changes in the industrial relations landscape in the 1960s and 1970s put HR in a new role of police officer to the labour relations process. It was not until the early 1980s that new approaches to the function gave rise to the concept of human resource management (HRM), which drew on two themes in the 1980s, both of which carry relevance today.

The first was an early attempt to link HR activity with business outcomes through the work of Charles Fombrum, Noel Tichy and Mary Anne Devanna[1], who developed a model of the HR cycle to show how key HR policies and activities could be linked to the delivery of business strategy. Although relatively unsophisticated by today's standards, the approach demonstrated that HR could have a direct influence on employee performance in support of organizational strategy.

The second view to emerge was the Harvard model, led by the work of Professor Michael Beer[2], which shifted the focus towards the consideration of the employee as a 'human resource', where the focus was shifted away from HR processes and systems and towards a model that sought to manage through developing high commitment amongst employees. This approach sought to align employee commitment at an individual level with the goals and strategies of the organization.

The implication of both approaches was that HR had the means to improve organizational performance, which, in turn, extended the range of activities that HR might legitimately become involved in and the information they demanded to manage such processes effectively.

From the systems and data perspective the emphasis moved, for the first time, away from payroll processing and manpower modelling towards consideration of the employee performance cycle and how that supported the delivery of organizational objectives. This period gradually saw the emergence of a lifecycle of activity against which HR could start to pin demands for data and system functionality to support new ways of working (see Figure 1.1).

The development of HR 'levers' to manage employee behaviours in support of organizational objectives highlighted a need for much improved management information and supporting processes in several areas.

---

1   See for example, *The Transformational Leader*, Tichy, N. and Devanna, M.A. (1997) (Wiley)
2   See *Managing Human Resources*, Beer, M. (1984) (Boston: Harvard University Press)

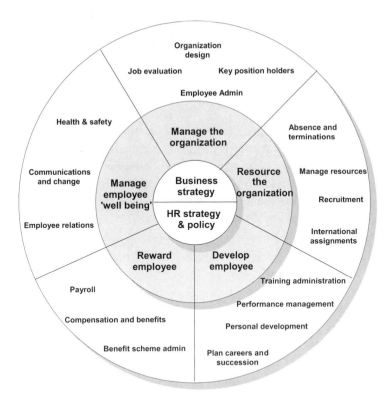

Figure 1.1   The performance cycle and demands on HR systems

Managing the organization: The human resource management vision first demanded knowledge of what the organization needed to fulfil its objectives. This gave rise to an increased focus on the organizational structure and the demands of specific roles within it; job evaluation gave more information about the job content of specific roles, whilst competency profiles could set out the precise behavioural demands of a successful employee in the role.

From a systems perspective, this demanded a significant new set of information to be held in an organizational record, distinct from that of the employee. This in turn could be used to drive several processes in HR as well as inform related processes outside HR (for example, the sharing of organizational hierarchy data could be used to inform both financial planning and procurement processes).

Resourcing the organization: The rise of HRM also gave focus to the resourcing process. Whilst, historically, HR held responsibility for the mechanics of recruitment, the discipline of resourcing demanded knowledge of how the requirements of the organization were made up and where those demands could best be sourced.

Thus organizations started to focus on their own resource pools and, from a systems perspective, saw the emergence of requirements to match employee capability to demands in the organization; specifically to focus on the 'gaps' between an employee's personal competency profile and the demands of a specific role.

At the same time, the recruitment function started to develop administrative systems that could support the manually intensive mechanics of the process, such as producing correspondence, processing CVs and assessing the effectiveness of different providers in the process, as well as the ever growing statutory demands around the monitoring and recording of workforce composition statistics.

Developing the employee: The process of highlighting where employees performance currently lay in relation to their roles and addressing any gaps then became a primary occupation for HR. Performance appraisal, performance management and training and development activity to bring employees to the levels of competence required for their roles became the principal levers for aligning employee performance with the objectives of the business.

This in turn created new demands on systems to hold data on the employee development process. As well as maintaining a competency profile, systems were needed to cope with the process of measuring employee performance. The appraisal process grew more formalized and time critical as it became imperative to complete the appraisal cycle to meet other development goals in the HR calendar.

At the same time, as with recruitment, managing administration of the process became burdensome unless systems could be developed to support the distribution of forms and correspondence and to collate and analyze results.

Rewarding the employee: Whilst not exclusively so, the performance lifecycle was frequently tied to reward management as the link between performance aligned with business objectives and the contents of the employee's pay packet.

O&M related payments had been common since the beginning of the century and hence provided little technical challenge to payroll systems. However, the need to extend this approach to a new generation of clerical/ managerial activities highlighted the need for HR systems that operated in a fully integrated manner to support the performance cycle.

This meant that all of the processes identified above needed to operate in a seamless manner, with data from one part of the process fully available to the next stage of the process without the need for re-keying data or shepherding data through a shaky set of technical interfaces.

As a minimum, systems were required to provide a clear, auditable trail showing the basis on which employees were rewarded, which in turn demanded a single view of the HR process and data and a level of integration between the component parts of the HR system that had seldom been seen before.

Geographical Factors

For large organizations, geography was frequently one of the major constraining factors in developing an integrated view of HR data and process. Figure 1.2, based on a real case study, demonstrates the organizational mix that many organizations need to deal with.

The delivery of HR services from multiple locations has frequently led to a wide mix in the processes and capabilities of the different regional operations. Organic growth of the both the company and the HR function have led to a fragmentation of the HR organization and the processes it carries out.

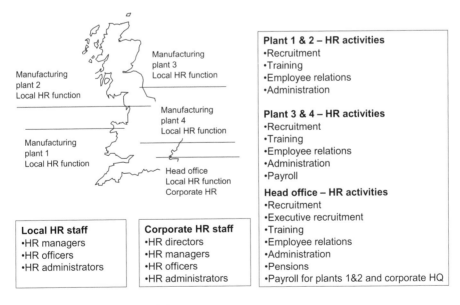

Figure 1.2   Geographical factors

Within this type of structure it is fairly common to find that, HR administration is carried out in several different locations, there are differences in the way the process is managed and the data that are recorded that make it impossible to develop a consolidated view of the organization. In such an environment, the 'simple headcount' question inevitably becomes a manual task that can occupy many hours of HR time.

For much of the last 20 years, the focus of HR system developers has been to tackle the integration of HR data and process from multiple locations. Differences of process were frequently accommodated through the use of data warehouses and translation tables to produce a meaningful set of data for use at corporate level.

Organizations selecting HR systems have frequently prized the flexibility of an application to adapt to such differences and present a relatively seamless view of data to the corporate centre. However, this is clearly doing little to address the more fundamental issue of the effectiveness of HR operations under these circumstances.

The Battle for Functionality

In order to meet this challenge, HR systems providers have had to dig deep to develop applications that can not only provide products which incorporate broad and best practice thinking, but are also effective in large and small organizations alike. In many respects the HR needs of most organizations are common: staff need to be hired, paid, and developed and so these processes must be delivered flawlessly. However the need to maintain competitive advantage requires the HR function to maintain a rapid pace of change. As a consequence, HR systems have to work alongside legacy systems, be sufficiently flexible to accommodate numerous variations in structure and process, and be scalable, efficient and cost effective.

The work engine of the HR system resides in its ability to manage administrative routines with all the transactional capability needed to support fundamental employee lifecycle events. Recruitment, from advertising through to selection and onboarding; the complete payroll service, from salary calculation in all its various forms through to statutory deductions and reporting; and learning and development administration, from course bookings through to competency frameworks and the performance management process. This latter area of functionality is quite rightly seen by the organization as the business end of HR and high levels of performance are expected. Failure to get this part right will negate any attempt by HR to earn a voice at the top table.

We have seen earlier in the chapter that the provision of management information has progressed from simply maintaining employee data to holding data at an organizational level, driving processes not only in HR but across the whole organization. HR systems must have the capability to provide the operational management information needed to support ongoing processes; the capability to generate tactical management information to enable the measurement of the overall HR performance and the effectiveness of policies, and most importantly the ability to provide strategic management information for use by the senior management in determining the progress of the business against its key performance indicators (management information is examined in more detail in Chapter 3).

Reporting tools themselves, previously the domain of IT, are now required to be in the hands of the users, whether in HR or the business. These are expected to be flexible and able to 'slice and dice' information routinely or speedily in bespoke fashion. Increasingly, line managers with access to self-service applications expect to be able to produce information for their own business unit not only in prewritten format but also using variable parameters, rather than having to ask for reports from HR. To achieve this, it is no longer acceptable for reporting tools to be so complex that only the limited few in HR can use them. The requirement is for reporting tools to be able to meet the needs not only of the expert user but also the HR professional and the line manager.

The issue of system integration affects functions across the whole organization, not just HR. We will see in Chapter 3 that the issue of integration touches the whole of the HR landscape. But it is critical that applications are able to fully integrate or to be successfully interfaced with other systems, generating all the benefit this brings in terms speed of implementation, costs, and sharing of common data structures and terminology. The evaluation of alternative products at selection stage will always highlight this issue as a major consideration, often triggering heated debate between the HR community, who understandably will be looking for richness of functionality, and IT, who will be concerned about cost and skills required to maintain systems as well as ensuring that any solution is consistent with company-wide IT strategy.

The marketplace for HR systems has evolved over the last decade from one dominated by the large enterprise-wide providers targeting mid to large organizations offering wide functionality and the benefit of integration with, for example, finance and procurement systems; and niche providers satisfying demand amongst smaller organizations, to the position where we are today, with many providers being able to offer HR products with functionality broad enough to satisfy the requirements of organizations of all sizes. Importantly, however, there remains a key differentiator – the ability of the product to integrate into the technology platform. This has resulted in providers being placed in one of two categories: Tier 1 – products which have a high degree of integration capability both across the organization and within HR itself, dominated by SAP and Oracle (Chapter 3 examines in detail the role of technology across the whole of the HR service centre); and Tier 2 – products with little integration capability, relying exclusively on interfaces between systems.

Whether Tier 1 or Tier 2 is right for the organization can only be decided by a thorough evaluation process, examining in detail all aspects of functionality, system capability, costs and many other factors, which will help determine the correct choice. Inevitably, there will be trade offs but if ever there was an example of the value of spending time up front weighing up the relevant issues before making an investment decision then the selection of a new system is perhaps the best. The construction of a business case is examined in more detail in Chapter 6.

Emergent HR Models and the Implications for Technology

We have explored the way that organizations demand more than professional competence from their HR functions, with the resultant increased reliance upon technology. HR functions are expected to be as operationally efficient as any other part of the business and in so doing exploit technology to improve the range and quality of service at speed and lower cost.

Whilst technology is a key enabler, it cannot be used in isolation from other changes and any HR function that believes that it alone will revolutionize the operation is deluding itself. Key stakeholders demand greater strategic capability, operational efficiency and all that is required to address the challenge that the new models of HRM pose. Dave Ulrich proposed a model that gave HR a focus to tackle these issues.

The Ulrich Model

In his book *Human Resource Champions*, Ulrich starts with the question 'should we do away with HR?'.[3] In the opening of his book, he suggests that we may have to if we cannot move the focus of HR from, for example, hiring, training

---

3   Ulrich, D. (1997), *Human Resource Champions; the Next Agenda for Adding Value and Delivery Results* (Boston, Mass., Harvard University Press), p. vii.

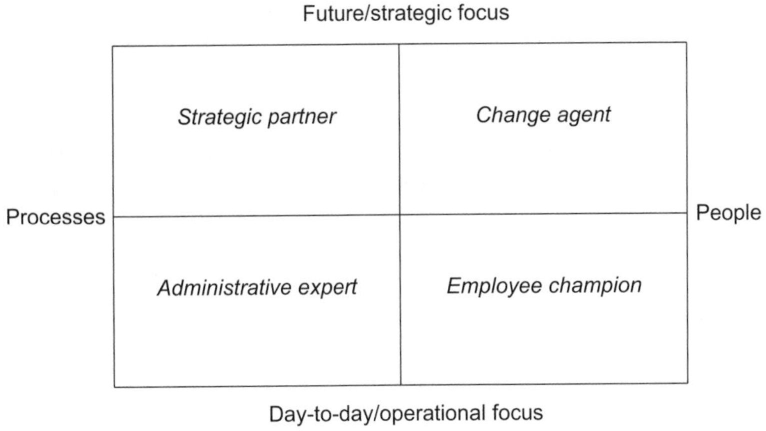

Future/strategic focus

Strategic partner	*Change agent*
Administrative expert	*Employee champion*

Processes

People

Day-to-day/operational focus

Figure 1.3   The Ulrich model

and payroll to how it delivers these services. This is a vital proposition. Ulrich proposes that HR should select four key areas of activity that, when executed well as a whole, will support HR's position and its ability to meet whatever challenges that may come along. Figure 1.3 above illustrates this point.[4]

Ulrich maps out new roles for HR. Each role combines to focus on delivering improvement within the function and within the business as set out in Table 1.1.[5]

Table 1.1   Linking Ulrich's roles to deliverables

Metaphor	Role	Activity	Deliverable
Strategic partner	Management of strategic resources	Aligning HR and business strategy	Executing strategy
Administrative expert	Management of firm's infrastructure	Re-engineering process	Building an efficient infrastructure
Employee champion	Management of employee contribution	Listening and responding to employees	Increasing employee commitment and capability
Change agent	Management of transformation and change	Managing transformation and change	Creating a renewed infrastructure

4   Ulrich has subsequently altered his model with the acknowledgement that in many organizations there still exists a role for operational HR to support the business.

5   Many of these themes are dealt with more thoroughly in our book *HR Business Partners*: Hunter, I., Saunders, J., Boroughs, A. and Constance, S. (2006), *HR Business Partners* (Aldershot, Gower).

Through Ulrich's model, HR is enabled to tackle the strategic issues by having a strategic business partner who focuses upon them. The administrative expert helps to demonstrate that HR is supporting the financial goals of the company by having an efficient and high quality service. The function is also able to focus on the employee relationship and improving employee capability through the establishment of the employee champion role. Finally, the change agent role allows the function to meet the challenges of the changing business environment and positioning the business to execute strategy.

HR technology is a key enabler in the execution of this strategy. Without the assistance of new technology in redesigning the way work is organized and managed within the HR function and allowing the delivery of service from remote locations, it is likely that the model would have little impact on transforming HR.

For the business partner, technology is a critical tool to support delivery and will govern their access to:

- critical HR management information to support business decisions;

- specialist data to support planning and development;

- the transactional service provided by the shared service centre (covered later in this chapter).

For the administrative expert, it provides the tools to:

- redesign processes and generate a 'step change' in service quality;

- exploit the delivery of services through multiple channels;

- deliver significant savings in the cost of delivering the HR service.

For the employee champion, it:

- gives direct access to all employees through self-service;

- enables direct feedback from employees on all areas of employment;

- empowers employees by giving them more control over managing their careers.

And for the change agent, it provides:

- strategic HR information to support decision making;

- the channels to effectively communicate with employees;

- a flexible infrastructure to enable the delivery of the new organization.

IMPLICATIONS FOR THE MODERN HR FUNCTION

The Ulrich model itself did not come with an 'out of the box' organizational structure for HR functions to adopt. Over time, a model has evolved with companies, which allows them a means to manage all of the relationships between employees and HR through a single channel: the shared service centre (SSC).

The Shared Service Centre

The SSC provides the focused administrative excellence that drives financial efficiency and HR credibility through the quality of its output, 'getting the basics right on time every time'.

The scope of the SSC will depend on the nature of the organization: its size, complexity, location, market and so on. But there are common elements that you would expect to see in all service centres, enabling consolidation of similar HR administrative activities from multiple business units into a single location, leveraging value from exploiting standardization and centralization opportunities. By doing this, the SSC is able to exercise greater control over transactional HR administrative activities, drive out costs and create a platform for the investment in new technologies. Figure 1.4 illustrates this model.

As can be seen from the diagram, the scope of the SSC embraces all of the administrative activities behind the core HR service lines (recruitment, performance management, training, employee relations, pay and benefits, pensions and leavers, information systems and vendor management). The service is delivered through multiple channels, including the web, e-mail and telephone, to offer the widest degree of access regardless of need, whether to employees, line managers or HR.

The initial entry point to the SSC is through the contact centre, sitting above the functional process teams and acting as the first contact point, only referring specialized or complex queries to the subject matter experts – ideally 80 per cent of e-mails and calls should be resolved at the first point of contact. The ability to resolve the vast majority of queries at the first point of contact generates the means to generate service levels to users and cost reduction opportunity for HR.

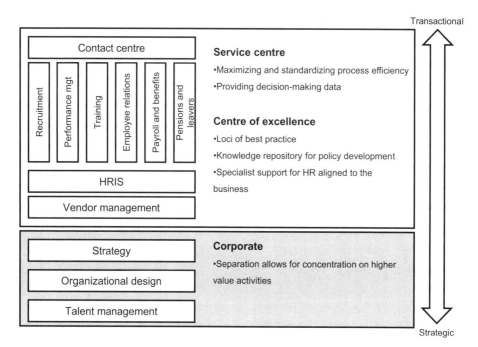

Figure 1.4   **The scope of HR activities carried out within the shared service centre, centre of excellence and the corporate centre**

The contact centre is also pivotal in providing support to the centres of excellence and business partner team by filtering enquiries, only allowing through those which require high level and specialist intervention (both functions are covered in more detail later in this chapter).

The design of the SSC is critical in order to realize its full potential particularly in the area of process design and capability to efficiently handle large transaction volumes. For example, a large financial institution with a mature shared service operation will routinely handle 12,000–15,000 recruits a year from around 100,000 applicants, 6,000 leavers, 3,000 staff on maternity leave, 25,000 calls a month through its contact centre and so on. To achieve this successfully at low cost and high performance levels demands not only the right technology supporting the right tasks but ensuring that processes are critically examined to minimize cycle times and, most importantly, integrated to avoid duplication.

Examples of the transactional activities carried out by service centres are numerous but looking at recruitment illustrates the importance of getting the process engineered correctly. The process for recruitment includes creating the vacancy, advertising, administering the applicant (tracking), interviewing, making the offer, checking references and so on. At each stage, applicant information is gathered that needs to be entered into the system not only to support the same process 'downstream', but to inform other processes; for example, ordering a company car, setting up the payroll record, organizing onboarding and training, pension administration and much more. Duplicate entry of data would clearly undermine any attempt to achieve improvements in operational efficiency. Similarly, attention to design detail at this stage is crucial to being able to monitor the performance of HR key performance indicators (KPIs) through system driven operational management information reporting.

HR functions now routinely use process re-engineering experts, usually but not always from outside the function, to support transformation projects with the added benefit of being seen to use the same tools as the rest of the business. Six Sigma and lean manufacturing techniques are the most commonly evidenced tools used today.

The benefits to the organization, if successfully exploited, are significant, allowing the business to focus more of its attention and resources on added value areas in the knowledge that back office administration is disciplined and under tight management oversight. Below are some of the frequently cited benefits from implementing a SSC:[6]

- drives down general and administrative costs;

- creates a clear relationship between cost and service;

- improves service levels and quality;

- maximizes technology investments.

The Centre of Excellence

It is critical that HR retains deep technical knowledge of the business within the aegis of the shared service environment. Compensation, benefits, employee relations as well as thorough familiarity with legacy policies and terms and conditions are typical examples of knowledge that has evolved within the HR function. The centre of excellence (CofE) is that part of the shared service function that holds these specialist skills, providing invaluable support to the business, but in particular to strategic business partners.

The scope of activities covered by the HR centre of excellence will vary according to the nature of the HR challenges faced by the business,

6   Quinn, B., Cooke, R. and Kris, A. (2000), *Shared Services, Mining for Corporate Gold* (London, Prentice Hall).

its size, complexity and geography. For example, in retail banking, those responsible for serious disciplinary and grievance cases will reside in the CofE. In a manufacturing environment, employee relations specialists will travel to local sites to provide on-hand advice and support. Activities are included in the scope of the CofE if they require deep process and technical knowledge.

The distinction between the SSC and the CofE is therefore quite clear: high-volume, service-orientated transactional capability versus specialist technical and professional advice and support. The types of activity most commonly found within a typical CofE are shown in Figure 1.5.

Further examples of the type of specialist activity found within the CofE are as follows:

- *Recruitment* – teams of recruiters who support and plan large-scale recruitment campaigns and who may deploy sophisticated assessment centre tools where local resource is either not available or insufficiently skilled.

- *Performance management* – individuals who are able to create policy and design advice to support local business units.

- *Training* – training design, specialist delivery resources and the management of relationships with specialist external providers.

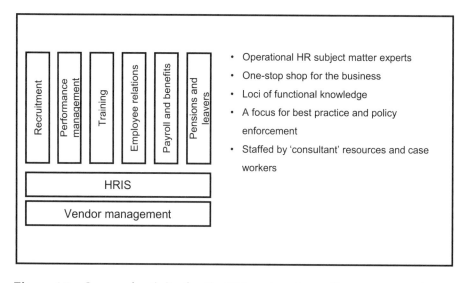

Figure 1.5   Scope of activity for the HR centre of excellence

- *Employee relations* – overall responsibility for managing union relationships within the business units as well as providing support in meeting legal and compliance responsibilities and in key elements of disciplinary, grievance, redundancy and sickness management processes.

- *Pay and benefits* – provides business specialist advice on reward policy, payroll, benefits and tax.

- *Pensions and leavers* – particularly relevant around pension policy formulation and complexities associated with merger and acquisition activities.

- *Information systems* – the extent of the capability held in the CofE depends on where accountability for maintenance lies – in HR or IT where full technical support could reside in either. As a minimum 'super users' would be needed as would the expertise to provide strategic manpower and succession planning and reporting.

- *Vendor management* – may be integrated within each of the CofE teams where deep subject knowledge is held or in a single team where specialist procurement skills can be exploited.

The adoption of a CofE generates a number of benefits:[7]

- experience in specialist areas can easily be accessed by the whole organization;

- learning can be shared across the experts;

- greater consistency can be achieved in interpreting policy for the business;

- expert staff can be more efficiently deployed.

The HR Business Partner

The Ulrich model requires the HR function to tackle each of the four quadrants individually, ensuring that appropriate skill sets are effectively deployed; each quadrant focuses on the activities that make it successful. From this it is necessary to align the HR roles necessary to implement the model, as illustrated in Figure 1.6.

As we have seen, each sector requires a distinct skill set to effectively operate with the HR business practices (BP) interacting across all elements of the model,

7   Quinn, B, Cooke, R and Kris, A (2000), *Shared Services, Mining for Corporate Gold* (Prentice Hall).

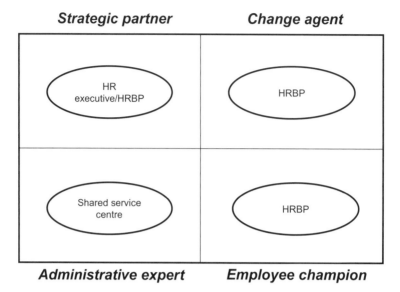

Figure 1.6   Roles in the Ulrich model

supported by each of these functions and the wider business as a whole. It is from this that organizations can determine what the role of the HR BP should actually look like. The HR BP role needs:

- the credibility to engage with the business;

- to be accepted into the management team to allow the HR BP to fully understand the strategic objectives and to influence key decisions with a people dimension;

- deep influencing, change and transition management skills that are traditionally associated with HR;

- to access the right support, technical and administrative, to enable it to deliver.

But what is the HR BP's role within the SSC model, and what does the role involve? Figure 1.7 examines a framework within which tasks can be allocated between the SSC and group or business unit HR, to complement and support the HR BP role.

From this it can be determined that the group HR BP role is centred primarily around setting strategic HR direction, determining policy, scanning externally for best practice and, importantly, advising the SSC on the implementation of policy and strategy. In contrast, the business unit HR BP

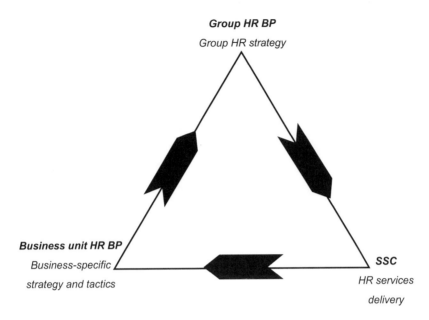

Figure 1.7   The relationship between group HR, the SSC and business unit HR BPs

is more involved in articulating business unit operational needs, providing hands on support, providing operational management information (hires, leavers and so on) and of course working alongside the SSC to deliver business requirements.

SUMMARY OF CHAPTER MESSAGES

- The developments in HR over the last ten years, driven by David Ulrich and others, have set a new agenda for HR technology. Transformation technology is no longer defined by traditional views of core HR systems, and a radically different range of technologies is required to meet the demands of the new model and its customers.

- In developing the new technology architecture, the functional capabilities of the system are considerably less important than the ability to integrate them into the wider architecture of the organization. A decade of rapid functional development has left many applications holding more capability than their customers can effectively use; however the ability to integrate data effectively and produce a coherent 'single version of the truth' is the major differentiator between successful and unsuccessful systems.

- Organizations that do not invest in developing legacy technologies will find it difficult to deliver the benefits of HR transformation. In the longer term, legacy systems will act as a barrier to change and may force the system to look at outsourced HR solutions where capital investment in applications may be amortized over several years.

The Evolution of HR Technology

How well is the HR function served by technology after 40 years of parallel evolution? Sadly our experience is that most organizations are caught in a continual process of 'technology tag': new developments in HR demand new approaches to HR computing, which in turn consume large amounts of time and budget whilst generally failing to deliver their promise.

While this is happening, the organization inevitably develops further, leading to demands for newer technology, and thus the cycle repeats. The result is that many HR organizations live with a patchwork quilt of technologies that chart the development of HR operations over many years but which add little value to the overall function.

The IT Legacy in HR

Examples of poor HR architectures abound: personnel records are frequently held in multiple locations and systems (perhaps the legacy of past mergers and acquisitions) which fail to provide a complete picture of the workforce; mainframe payrolls sit alongside PC-based reward systems and are unable to share common data; web-based recruitment tools invite applications on an international scale, which cannot be shared or distributed within the organization.

Clearly this is not true in all organizations. Many enterprises on widely differing scales have successfully developed HR tools that serve the purpose of the HR organization without becoming a constraint on the ability to change. The development of complete and integrated HR data and effective management information in turn creates the climate for developing new service led models for HR delivery.

What is the difference between the two models? How are some organizations able to leverage technology effectively in HR whilst others have inherited a fragmented selection of applications that offer limited strategic value?

Evolution of the HR Application Market

To understand the nature of current problems with HR technology, it is necessary first to understand something of how HR technology solutions have evolved. Many of the problems routinely encountered in HR systems have their roots in design and development problems that relate to older technologies and which no longer need be a constraint on the organization.

Throughout this chapter we have referenced the major stages in the historical development of HR technologies in the boxes detailing the *History of HR Technology*, which should be read in parallel with the points made here.

THE PAYROLL-DRIVEN SOLUTION

The beginnings of HR technology arose with the need to process large numbers of employee payslips which, prior to the 1960s, was predominantly a manual or clerical exercise. The advent of large mainframe applications to process payroll calculations and generate paper payslips on a large scale was, for most organizations, the first major application of technology to an HR-related problem.

Such systems rapidly proved their value in reducing clerical activity and the number of staff required to support the process within both finance and HR. At the same time it was recognized that such payroll systems often held a useful repository of employee information, including data about jobs, pay, cost, absence levels and personal data. This stimulated demand for better information and quickly led to the development of HR-related applications that held additional management information on individual employees that could, for the first time, be used to produce meaningful information on which to base strategic decisions in the function.

At this point the 'market' for HR systems was split fairly evenly between organizations that built their own systems, often employing large IT armies to do this for them, and a small embryonic group of HR system vendors (in the UK this included vendors such as Peterborough Software, Midland, Dun and Bradstreet and Cyborg).

It was a testament to the quality of some of the solutions produced at this time that many are now still in use in some organizations and at least three of the above software vendors are still in existence in some form. However, as HR information needs developed, mainframe technologies quickly proved to be a constraint.

History of HR Technology

MAINFRAME SOLUTIONS

The earliest forms of HR systems were the large mainframe-based payroll solutions used to process large volumes of routine pay calculations quickly and efficiently. It was realized early on that the basic personal data used to manage payroll could be easily extended to support equally basic personnel records. Names, addresses, job titles and other basic employment data could be held alongside payroll records and, with the application of some reporting tools, could start to produce limited statistics on the employee population. This early stage was dominated by names such as Peterborough Software, Midland Software, Dun and Bradstreet and Cyborg Systems, many of whom still exist today, albeit in different incarnations.

The mainframe system had many advantages: for many organizations it was the first experience of automating the management of employee data, and the efficiency savings were significant. Mainframe computers themselves were significant assets in the organization and were managed in a rigorous and centralized manner. They offered little flexibility, and making changes tended to be a complex and difficult process; access to HR data was restricted by security systems but also by the accessibility of a suitable mainframe terminal.

Much of this suited the HR (or personnel) functions in large organizations of the time as they too tended to be centrally focused and steeped in routine transactional operations that changed little over time. HR systems existed to support the HR function and the concept of sharing data outside the function was not widely known.

Whilst mainframe systems are, by their nature, very adept at sharing data across a wide network and maintaining a secure and robust environment, at the outset of the business computing era mainframe systems tended to be highly inflexible and heavily dependent on skilled technical resources who could build required applications. At this point the relationship between HR and IT was often characterized by a harassed end user attempting to explain to a white-coated 'techie' what was required.

With such a focus on the technical difficulties of delivery, it was not surprising that the developed solutions were cumbersome, expensive to build and maintain, difficult to use and, generally, did not deliver what was needed.

HUMAN RESOURCE MANAGEMENT SYSTEMS – EVOLUTION OF THE DEDICATED HR SYSTEMS MARKET

The development of the personal computer and related trends in computing such as client-server architectures unleashed a whole new set of computing possibilities for HR. The flexibility and local processing capability offered by PCs meant that HR users could maintain their own HR records and information and could quickly generate the types of specialized management information that would previously have required dedicated technical resources. Whilst PC systems were easy to acquire and operate, they had a significant downside in that they tended to lack any real integration with the payroll system or indeed any other business applications. Therefore whilst PC systems offered significant advantages, their stand-alone nature led to a host of new problems in terms of keeping HR systems in step with other data.

Client-server architectures offered the potential to share this information across a wider network and to distribute data processing, data storage and presentation to the end user across different technical platforms according to the requirements of the task. At the same time, more advanced database and reporting tools, particularly the advent of fourth generation languages such as Oracle, provided far more flexibility to structure and analyze data in a way that was less dependent on the restrictive hierarchical data structures found in mainframe systems.

These changes in the options for technology delivery provided the catalyst the industry required to develop a new generation of HR specific systems and tools. Software vendors rapidly evolved applications to manage the complexities of HR processes such as historical record keeping, time and labour recording, organizational management, performance management, recruitment administration and a whole host of other functional areas. With the development of new functions, businesses started to recognize the possibilities and quickly wanted to tailor the new systems to meet unique or specialized requirements in their own organizations; thus the requirement for flexible business solutions was created.

New systems were generally delivered with a set of configuration tools that would allow the organization to make subtle (and sometimes not so subtle) changes to the core system to meet their local requirements. This in turn demanded a specialist set of skills to manage the implementation of the new system.

Vendor marketing messages focused on how technology solutions would provide the basis for a revolution in the way HR was managed in the organization, and a race began between the main vendors to develop functionality that would differentiate their system from their competitors'.

However, whilst the new systems and architectures offered considerable advantages they also opened up a wide range of complexity around HR solutions that brought a whole new set of problems. Because the applications market for HR was evolving so rapidly, many 'leading edge' products were

History of HR Technology

THE PERSONAL COMPUTER (PC) ERA

The advent of desktop PCs in the 1980s saw an explosion in the availability of cheap, flexible PC-based HR applications that were easy to install and offered a whole range of flashy reporting tools and functionality.

HR users were introduced to the possibility of managing much of their administration via a desktop system that would prepare standard letters, format sophisticated reports and support a range of functions such as succession planning and performance management that could not be attempted via a mainframe system.

The availability of such local processing power was a massive leap forward and many organizations still successfully use such solutions. However, in a pre-web era, the limitations of PC connectivity made it difficult to share data and the PC was effectively limited to operating in one location. In a distributed organization this rapidly led to a computing free-for-all with many different users developing their own desktop tools and databases, which inevitably did not agree with each other and which led to a high level of manual effort to reconcile systems.

Thus in early iterations, the enhanced functionality of the PC solution came at the cost of the integration offered by mainframe applications. However, the advent of web-based technologies and client-server architectures (see below) changed the scope of activity deployed on PCs and has opened the potential to manage HR process at the local level via employee and manager self-service. The PC HR solution has changed radically since its inception but is now a major component of the overall HR systems architecture.

rapidly eclipsed by developments from rival vendors. For the organization wishing to buy an HR solution, this often meant a comprehensive and lengthy evaluation process to determine which system best fit their needs.

In addition, many of the new systems were IT platform specific (for example running only on IBM, HP or Dec hardware), which meant that the evaluation process often boiled down to a debate between IT and HR about technical platform versus functional needs.

Once the preferred system was selected, organizations often found their problems were only beginning. The flexibility of new systems was a new-found freedom for HR users used to being told what was not possible. The ability to adapt systems was frequently interpreted as 'we can tailor the system to do whatever we want', which in turn led the systems delivery project down a route of complex and costly development projects that only succeeded in delivering a system that did what the old system did.

What was often lacking from such projects was any clear understanding of what opportunities the new system presented for streamlining existing process or how embedded process inherent in the system provided a basis for understanding and developing best practice processes. In addition, few business users were aware that tailoring an IT system was often a far more costly proposition than changing the process to fit the system.

From an IT perspective, the new technologies were often long on promise and short on delivery. PC systems proliferated as users discovered the advantage of personal computing power. However, in a pre-web environment, PCs were notoriously poor at sharing data, and systems integration became a major headache.

In a networked environment, the management of client-server solutions was frequently highly complex and beset by proprietary tools and systems that required a wide range of skills to implement. IT departments often resorted to imposing mainframe-like restrictions on the development of new systems in a deliberate attempt to limit the technologies they would need to support.

As HR solutions developed, therefore, the complexities on both the business and IT sides of the project frequently caused problems during delivery. Many high-profile delivery projects during this period floundered and successful systems delivery was often a hit and miss affair.

ERP/WEB-BASED APPLICATIONS

The development of integrated HR solutions was given further impetus by the emergence in the 1990s of enterprise resource planning (ERP) applications, such as Oracle, SAP and PeopleSoft. Initially the term was coined to describe a complete set of business applications that would cover all aspects of an organization's core processes, although later it generally came to mean applications that specifically focused on back office operations including HR, finance and procurement.

The development of an integrated approach to the back office meant the potential to eliminate the complexities of integrating cross-functional processes such as the management of organization structures (where HR and finance information seldom agreed) and paved the way for fully integrated solutions that might cover multiple back office processes and geographies.

At the same time, the introduction of web-based technologies meant that the historical problems relating to the sharing of data and processes over a network could now be managed by means of a universal set of technology tools. This in turn meant that anyone in the organization with access to a PC and an Internet connection could now use self-service tools that enabled line managers

History of HR Technology

CLIENT-SERVER ARCHITECTURES AND THE WEB

'Client-server' is a term that refers to a network architecture whereby there is a separation of the system which interacts with the end user (the client) from the system that manages the bulk of the heavy lifting work (the server).

The benefits of such an architecture are that it allows each machine in the network to perform the task to which it is best suited, with powerful servers managing the application software and database and desktop PCs taking care of the presentation and manipulation of data to the end user.

This translates into significantly better performance than would be experienced via a PC solution alone, whilst at the same time providing far greater power to drive more sophisticated applications. At the same time, the client-server approach also allows a potentially limitless number of users to access and manage the same data from different points on the network.

For HR this architecture promised to resolve many of the drawbacks of previous generations of HR technology by providing connectivity between hardware platforms and ensuring that users had access to the systems they needed.

In early incarnations, however, the principal drawback lay in the cost and complexity of the underlying architecture and the applications that were designed to run on them, as well as performance issues on process-hungry applications like payroll. More than one organization incurred massive costs trying to initiate a client-server solution without delivering any functionality to the user whatsoever.

The development of web-based tools meant that the principles of client server architecture could be deployed on a common platform over the Internet. Examples can be seen in a wide range of routine Internet transactions where an HTTP server provides information (typically a web page) to a client PC that requests access via a web browser using a standard Internet protocol.

The introduction of web-based self-service tools in a business environment mirrored users' personal experiences of Internet shopping or banking and has rapidly become a standard approach to delivering HR processes.

Although this approach brings significant benefits over earlier solutions, the transition has not been straightforward for all software providers, in particular:

- There can be a large variation in how applications manage the PC end of application – some systems still require a significant amount of code to be installed on a client PC to use self-service effectively, which can have implications for maintainability, support, upgrade and performance of the system.

- There are still big variations in opportunity of self-service tools – many software providers in the HR market have made rapid entry with 'web enabled' solutions, which offer very little flexibility to change these tools – users may find they are limited to what they can deploy via self-service.

and employees to access and update records and processes that, hitherto, had been the preserve of the HR function alone. It was the development of such fully integrated toolsets that made the organization of transactional activity into service centres and the reduction in administrative headcount a real possibility.

Through the course of the 1990s, three giants emerged in the vendor market as the main suppliers of such applications: SAP, Oracle and PeopleSoft; all three remain in a dominant position in the HR systems market, although PeopleSoft is now in the ownership of Oracle.

It was quickly apparent that the problems that had been experienced to date in delivering large-scale solutions needed to be addressed and the focus turned towards the techniques and methods used to implement these systems if such solutions were to be seen as credible and reliable. This period heralded the growing market in organizations specializing in systems integration and offering a wide variety of structured methodologies and preconfigured solutions. However, the fact remains that implementation remains the most problematic aspect of system.

'TOOLS ON TOP' – THE BEST-OF-BREED ARGUMENT

During the period of explosive growth in HR systems in the 1980s and 1990s, a new systems market emerged providing technology to meet specialist functional requirements. This market included a range of systems that were specifically designed to meet the needs of specialists in the HR field such as recruiters or trainers.

The rationale for such systems arose from the realization that an HR system that tried to cover all processes would inevitability lead to some compromise in the functionality offered. Specialist systems, it was argued, could bring a unique focus on providing 'best-of-breed' functionality based on expert knowledge. The argument quickly took hold, particularly in organizations that had a critical focus in areas not adequately catered for by the mainstream HR systems and it rapidly became the norm to supplement a core HR solution with additional package functionality from other suppliers with some organizations even building their entire HR systems architecture from best-of-breed packages.

Best-of-breed solutions undoubtedly have an important place in the overall architecture for any organization; for example, an organization faced with a need for high-volume recruitment in an industry with strong competition for new recruits may need to invest in more comprehensive tools to manage the process than may be available from the mainstream suppliers. The difficulty can arise when trying to integrate data from the specialist systems with data from the core systems.

Orion Partners frequently encounter organizations that have invested in a wide range of specialist technologies to manage their HR processes but have failed to make similar investments in ensuring that these technologies can share data effectively. Too late, many find out that, in buying specialist tools to support critical processes around resourcing, learning and development, performance management and reward, they have lost the ability to get a single view of the data and manage these processes in a coordinated fashion. Thus the ideal of leading edge functionality is often outweighed by a practical need to integrate core HR data, which, in our experience, is the more important of the two requirements.

Impact of the New HR Model

The emerging web-based technologies from ERP and best-of-breed vendors paved the way for a reorganization of back office processes and the opportunity to devolve process and activity to its point of origin in the organization by means of self-service tools.

The work of David Ulrich and others demonstrated the impact that shared service centres (SSCs) could have on service cost and quality and prompted many organizations down this route. The shared service centre carried many of the requirements of a traditional HR operation but also created new demands for contact management, service monitoring and control and financial recharging that were new to HR operations.

EMERGING ROLES

The new model brought new roles such as HR business partners (HR BPs) and centres of expertise, who emerged as specialists who would, naturally, develop their own demands for management information and systems to support their roles (see Figure 2.1).

For example, the focus in the SSC on customer services, key performance indicators (KPIs) and cost performance drove a demand for systems to support:

- contact management, to monitor and manage service delivery at the point of contact with employees;

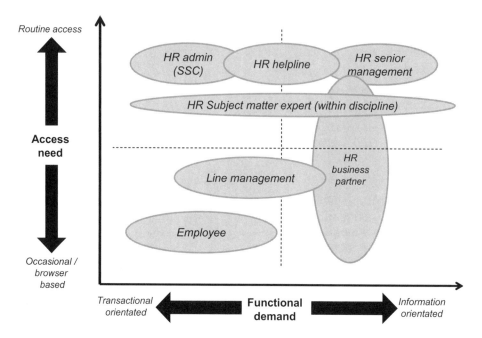

Figure 2.1   New roles influence demands on HRIS

- strongly integrated end-to-end processes for core transactions;

- performance monitoring systems that provide effective metrics to measure and improve the service.

For the HR BPs and subject matter experts, the emphasis will likely be on the development of a coherent and reliable source of data that can drive predictive trend analysis from historical data. Particular questions the HR BP may wish to resolve include:

- predicting seasonal peaks in business demand for HR services as a basis for planning HR delivery strategy;

- accurate historical data on individual performance, reward and terms and conditions to support organization design decisions;

- providing data on external benchmarks and comparators;

- tools to support the development of scorecard metrics.

Most importantly, however, the evolution of HR technology had taken systems out of the sole preserve of HR and placed them firmly at the heart of business operations. Now a new set of demands and standards are emerging

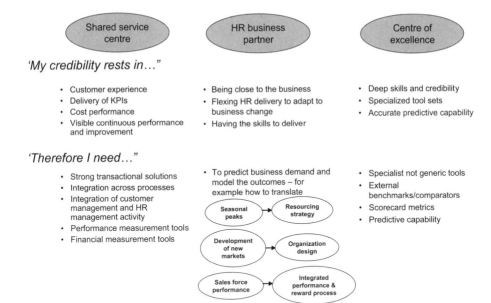

Figure 2.2   What drives performance in the new HR model?

from business users of HR data who understand the importance of a single source of HR data to support multiple processes across the organization.

Requirements can be as varied as the organizations that generate them, but there is an increasing realization of the value of HR data to critical business processes and planning. For example, the construction industry has seen massive growth in the UK over recent years: retail expansion, a booming property market and the countdown to the London Olympics have led to a significant demand for scarce construction resources, high staff turnover and full employment amongst skilled workers.

Against this background, there is increasing realization that historical approaches to planning construction project resource requirements and managing project staff costs using informal, local planning systems relying on estimated data simply won't do. Such organizations need to make maximum effective use of their human capital and therefore are increasingly reliant on a common source of HR and finance data to support resourcing and costing decisions.

THE DEMAND FOR INTEGRATION

For the HR organization developing a technical strategy to support the new HR model, this inevitably means considering tools and systems that were previously outside their domain. The use of contact management and customer relationship management (CRM) systems to monitor contact and service centres has now become standard practice in HR SSC operations. In addition, HR technology increasingly needs to include within its scope the use of telephony, document imaging and work management tools. The need for continuous improvement and service level monitoring has placed new emphasis on performance metrics and balanced scorecard reporting, and the move to commercial management of HR operations has driven a requirement for information to monitor transactional activity and manage the formal recharging of services.

The demand for integration therefore extends beyond the historical view of a requirement for integrated HR and payroll operations. New HR technologies have to address the need for integration on several levels:

- *Cross-functional integration within HR*: Whether or not HR systems are sourced from a single supplier or multiple best-of-breed vendors, there is a critical demand for related processes to share a common view of data and drive a seamless process. Performance management, reward management and learning and development are prime examples of three areas which are closely interrelated and where any fragmentation of the underlying data will impact HR's ability to deliver effectively in any one area.

- *Cross-functional integration outside HR*: Similarly, there is a need to consider how HR data will work in conjunction with other business applications, particularly back office applications such as finance and procurement. A common point of contact between these three applications is the organization structure; specifically the data HR holds on the organization is reflected in finance (expressed in the chart of accounts) and in procurement (as authorities to purchase). Unless these applications are designed with the ability to integrate this data, the organization will be required to maintain the same organizational data several times over.

- *Integration of channel technologies where the demands of the shared service centre require a range of different systems to work in close cooperation*: Contact management systems, HR system, telephony tools, work management solutions and document management all need to work together effectively in a SSC if process optimization and improved service levels are to be realized.

- *eBusiness systems*: Whilst self-service systems may be integral to the core HR system, there may equally be a number of legacy web-based applications (for example, flexible benefits solutions or expenses systems) that lie outside the core and which need to work as part of the integrated process. Similarly there may be several repositories of HR policy data on existing intranet sites that may form part of the information base for the contact centre and which may require knowledge management tools to extract and present data as part of the contact centre's tool kit for answering caller queries.

- *Reporting requirements*: With such a wide range of technologies, careful consideration needs to be given to reporting requirements across the different sources of data. Standard reporting tools offered by an HR solution supplier may not offer the best solution to reporting across multiple platforms and the service centre architecture should include consideration of whether a data warehouse may be required to drive management information.

CHANGING ROLE FOR SOFTWARE VENDORS?

For HR systems suppliers, therefore, the battleground has shifted away from the development of new and better functional solutions. The functional 'arms race' has led to a position whereby the majority of users of the main ERP solutions are unable to make effective use of the full range of functionality offered to them; many are simply buying more system functionality than they can use.

Of far greater importance now to the emerging models of HR is the need for effective integration of core HR applications with the wider set of technology tools that are required to manage an HR SSC. Software vendors need to demonstrate that they possess an understanding of how a single end-to-end process will be supported by the technology and how the components of their product offerings fit together to provide a seamless suite of applications for shared services.

Sadly this is still a challenge to many suppliers who may not have had to make their products work this way before. For example, contact management solutions are an essential part of SSC technology; however, suppliers have frequently evolved their CRM tools to do a different job – namely to manage relationships with external customers – and still do not recognize the significance of these applications to HR.

We see ample evidence that many market-leading suppliers are still focused on products that meet the demands of the 'old' model of HR delivery where the emphasis is solely on core process and HR-related management information. As long as this focus remains then suppliers will not provide adequate support to the needs of the new model for an integrated set of technology to support shared services. Put simply – many suppliers are still focused on selling and shipping software models rather than building business solutions.

Against this background, the onus is clearly on the buyer of technology solutions to validate how and where a vendor's solutions have been delivered as an integrated solution for shared service.

CAPABILITY NOT FUNCTIONALITY

Given the historical complexities of implementation and the sometimes very public disasters that have been incurred, together with the growing complexity of IT solutions for HR, organizations would be well advised to place much greater emphasis in future on low cost, low risk, practical methods of delivering HR systems safely. Our research indicates very clearly that the greatest single drive of project success lies in the skills and capabilities of the project leadership team. By contrast, multiple experiences have shown that comprehensive software selection exercises simply demonstrate that there is little to choose between the main vendors in terms of the capabilities of their systems.

For the organization embarking on an HR systems delivery the message is clear: time spent on software selection will not yield a significant return in terms of project outcomes. Whilst differences remain between the main solutions, projects rarely fail because the underlying software lacks functional capability. What does make a far more significant difference to project outcome is the quality of project management and a sound approach to implementation.

Despite this, it is still common to find organizations investing several weeks, if not months, undergoing a detailed system evaluation at the expense of investing in the capabilities of the individuals who will support the process. The expansion in scope of applications that touch the HR service model demands a comprehensive and systematic approach to delivery and a focus on the capabilities of the team who will be responsible for making it happen.

SYSTEM GOVERNANCE

Effective technology delivery is still only part of the story in driving benefits from HR systems. Our experience of HR technology audits demonstrates that the problems with legacy systems often relate to problems with the governance of the solution as opposed to the technical implementation or support.

Problems frequently arise post implementation when management responsibility for the system is passed to a relatively junior 'super user', whose role centres on system housekeeping and report production duties. Worse, this role may be passed to a technical support person with limited HR business context.

Whilst the new system may be planned and delivered very effectively, there may be a natural pressure over time to introduce new functional or regional requirements that need to be met by supplementary systems or by customization or future developments to the core system. The system governance role is vital to protect the investment in technology and ensure it is not watered down over time. This does not mean blocking future developments but ensuring there is a business-focused review of any future requirements and that changes are carried out in the context of the benefits they will bring.

Specific duties of the governance role may include, but are not limited to, the following:

- ensuring future development of systems does not compromise the 'single version of the truth', that is, that future developments do not fragment data in core HR areas;

- evaluating proposals for new requirements to determine whether these can be met by the core application; generally requirements for add-on functionality or specialist tools should be resisted unless it is apparent these cannot be met (at least to a high degree) by the existing technology;

- maintaining the overall integrity of the solution as it is rolled out in other regional or operational areas.

Conclusion

Whilst past approaches to HR systems have focused predominantly on the product capabilities, success in the new model will be heavily dependent on the understanding and capabilities of the individuals involved. The delivery of complex business change projects associated with transition to SSC will demand a varied set of skills which will need to encompass:

- building a business focus into the design of services and systems and determining how the HR technology model will integrate with the overall design for HR;

- integrating organizational and process design in HR with the embedded capabilities of the solution;

- developing a technology model that combines proven solutions into an integrated whole;

- focusing on critical project factors such as the skills and capabilities of the project management team;

- managing mundane project elements such as data conversion and data cleansing, which have a disproportionate impact on project success;

- managing change and communications.

In Part II of this book we will explore exactly how new technologies are being integrated into a common platform to support the new HR model and the most effective approaches for delivery.

SUMMARY OF CHAPTER MESSAGES

- The evolution of HR systems has forced many organizations into a persistent game of 'catch up' to adapt to the latest developments.

- However, the functional 'arms race' perpetrated by software vendors is now largely defunct – evidence shows most organizations successfully deploy less than 25 per cent of the functionality they acquire.

- Evidence also suggests that project leadership and programme management capability are far more reliable indicators of project success than choice of software.

- This suggests organizations should focus less on lengthy software evaluation processes and more on evaluation and secondment of the skills and capabilities to deliver the project.

- The capabilities of ERP technologies for HR provide the foundation for change in the HR function. However, integration of a wider set of technologies is critical to success, and vendors must be able to demonstrate that they understand the business need and can offer a proven, integrated solution.

- Effective, business-focused governance of the HR IT solution is critical to protect investment in the HR IT and ensure the solution does not become fragmented/watered down over time.

- Emerging roles in HR will drive new requirements outside the traditional remit of HR including:

  - contact management;

  - knowledge management tools;

  - document management and telephony;

  - development of HR metrics and scorecard analyses;

  - specialist tools and external comparator data.

PART II
Core HR Technologies for the New Model

Technology in the HR Service Centre

In the previous chapter we saw how the adoption of a shared services model is a vital component of HR function transformation. HR shared service centres (SSCs) are highly complex operations that require extensive automation if they are to function with enough efficiency to deliver HR transformation objectives. This has led to the emergence of a range of additional systems beyond the traditional HRIS/payroll technology, all of which must be integrated to achieve maximum efficiency. An example of a comprehensive and integrated HR SSC technology architecture is shown in Figure 3.1.

HR has traditionally been regarded as a back-office function because it services an organization's staff rather than its external customers. However, as mentioned previously, the new service ethos within functions such as HR requires staff to be treated with exactly the same care and attention as external customers. As a result, as Figure 3.1 shows, the emergent HR SSC may itself now be divided into a customer-facing front office and a more transaction-oriented back office.

As a process progresses through the HR front office and into the back office, the supporting technology becomes less generic and more HR-specific. From a systems perspective, the HR front office comprises the channel technology layer used by HR's customers to communicate with the HR SSC, and the CRM layer which manages these contacts and the resultant work. The HR back-office layers comprise the more traditional HR applications – HRIS, payroll and a variety of specialist add-on systems (often referred to as 'tools on top').

There is also a management information (MI) component to HR technology that exists alongside each layer and in consolidated form across the whole model.

The main distinction between this architecture and more traditional HRIS/payroll-centric platforms is the CRM system. The CRM allows each channel

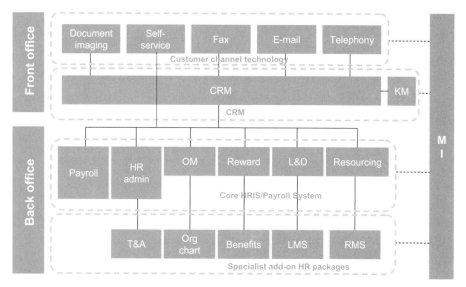

Figure 3.1   HR SSC technology

technology to be integrated with the HR systems architecture and each customer contact to be recorded, routed, progressed and monitored. These facilities allow far slicker and more comprehensive servicing of HR customers within a fully automated HR SSC compared to the more traditional HR operation.

In summary, the CRM delivers a new type of architecture, which changes the role of the other technology layers. The remainder of this chapter will consider each of these layers, including integration within and between them.

Customer Channel Technologies

As stated above, a variety of communication channels are available within an HR SSC – paper, e-mail, fax, telephony and so on. Each of these channels is described below, together with their supporting technology and how they can be integrated with the CRM to deliver process efficiencies. Before doing this, two qualifications are needed:

- Not all channels may be required – for example, some HR SSCs do not permit contact by e-mail because they consider that e-mails are too vague and unstructured, and will in any event require follow-up by telephone.

- Even if a channel is required, it may be decided not to have an automatic interface from the channel to the CRM – for example, an organization may consider that a telephony–CRM interface will not deliver a sufficiently personal customer experience for its own staff and managers.

DOCUMENT IMAGING

A fully automated HR SSC is a paperless environment. To achieve this, a series of steps must be applied to incoming documents:

- They are firstly scanned into image format by a scanning team.

- The image is then stored and indexed within an electronic document and records managements system (eDRMS). This involves attaching enough data to the document image (known as 'metadata', that is, data about data) to enable it to be accessed and manipulated both by the eDRMS itself, and the CRM (via an interface – see below). The metadata is likely to comprise a unique document identifier, its name (for example, MAT B1), the employee number to whom the document relates and the type of transaction (for example, maternity).

- The indexing details are then passed automatically by the eDRMS to the CRM by an interface between the two systems, which, depending on each product, may need to be developed or may come supplied with pre-written and configurable interfaces between the two products known as 'adaptors'. When the document's details reach the CRM, the interface program automatically opens a service request, which is a piece of work requiring action by an HR agent. The way in which the CRM is used to allocate and manage the work will be covered in the CRM section below.

Thus the CRM holds indexing details about the document, but not the actual document image itself, which remains on the eDRMS. However, when the document needs to be retrieved and displayed within the CRM by an HR agent, this can be achieved in real time via a second interface between the CRM and eDRMS. The key to this is that both systems are wholly web-enabled. This allows the document image to be directly accessed by the CRM from within the eDRMS via a 'web services' interface using the document's indexing data. Again, this interface will need to be developed if adaptors are not supplied with either product.

Some CRM suppliers offer their own eDRMS facilities, which, if selected for use, would obviate the interfacing requirement. However, the decision to use these facilities would depend upon the quality of the eDRMS and its fit with the organization's IT architecture.

FAX

At worst, an inbound fax from a customer can be scanned and indexed into the eDRMS as with ordinary incoming paper documents, and then interfaced as described above for access within the CRM. Depending upon the CRM's level of fax integration and/or its eDRMS capability, further automation may be possible, to a point where the faxed document could be transmitted direct to the CRM and a case created without human intervention.

SELF-SERVICE

Self-service is increasingly important in the delivery of the new HR service model. The ability to devolve HR tasks to employees and the line, thereby streamlining the work by automation, is a key contributor to delivering efficiency savings in the HR SSC. From the HR function's standpoint, the work previously undertaken by HR administrators upon receipt of forms completed by staff or the line manager is no longer necessary. For their part, the line manager or employee are merely entering on screen the same data that they had previously been completing manually, so they should be no worse off.

Self-service falls into two categories – view-only and update. For example, members of staff might use employee self-service (ESS) to view their payslips or a list of training courses, while a manager might use manager self-service to examine an absence report or an HR policy on line. Update access would be used to allow an employee to request overtime and a manager to approve it.

Although self-service comes as standard via HR/payroll systems, some organizations may wish to route self-service through the CRM, particularly if they feel that the CRM allows a more user-friendly front end, for example via the use of flexible electronic forms ('e-forms'). One advantage of this is that a record of all contacts, including Level 0, is available within the CRM for MI purposes, for example, highlighting where a particular benefit is attracting abnormal levels of interest. Against this must be balanced the need to create a set of web services interfaces between the CRM and each back-office system to allow the data to be available to self-service users via the CRM. These may be complex to develop, particularly when allowing data to be updated via the CRM rather than merely viewed.

E-MAIL

Email traffic into the CRM is managed by a standard interface between the email system and the CRM which allows a new CRM contact record to be generated for action by an HR agent when the email reaches the CRM's email inbox. The customer may be required to include the contact reference number on any subsequent email, so that the new contact can easily be added to or associated with the previous one. Outbound emails can be generated via the CRM as work on the query progresses, their contents being stored in the CRM for permanent record. Some HR SSCs choose not to allow contact by email because the content is too unstructured and may result in email 'to-ing and fro-ing' in order to clarify the precise nature of the query, after which a phone call may still be needed anyway. One compromise is to require email traffic to be conducted using more structured electronic forms ('eforms').

TELEPHONY

An HR SSC will require comprehensive private branch exchange (PBX) telephone system functionality, supplemented by a range of additional call centre telephony features.

Private Branch Exchange (PBX) Functionality

A private branch exchange (PBX) is an organization's internal telephone system. PBXs offer a range of capabilities including call transfer, customized abbreviated dialing, voicemail, follow-me, call forwarding on absence or busy, music on hold, automatic ring back, call waiting, call pick-up, call park, call conferencing and so on. In addition to these standard features, call centres generally and HR SSCs specifically are likely to require additonal telephony facilities, as described below.

Automatic Call Distribution (ACD)

Automatic call distribution (ACD) systems are used to route incoming calls to groups of agents, in cases where a caller has no need to talk to a specific person, but merely wishes to be connected to the first available agent. The system consists of hardware for the terminals and switches, phone lines, and software for the routing strategy. Having concluded one call, agents are able to indicate to the system that they are either available to receive another call or they are not ready, for example, because they are due to take a break.

ACD is an essential requirement for HR SSCs where pre-routing of callers according to the nature of their query is not generally necessary, that is, where all front line agents are expected to be able to field most HR queries irrespective of what they are about.

Interactive Voice Response (IVR)

Interactive voice response (IVR) allows the caller to feed data into the ACD's routing software by providing basic data about the reason for the call. To achieve this the system prompts the user via a pre-recorded voice to select from a menu of options. The user can make a choice either by pressing a number on the telephone keypad or speaking simple answers such as 'yes', 'no', or saying numbers in answer to the voice prompts.

IVR is often considered to be too impersonal for HR SSCs. Many organizations prefer initial contact to be with a 'warm' human voice, particularly where the agent is capable of dealing with most queries. Even where there may be a case for routing all enquiries on a particular topic (for example, pensions) straight through to a specialist second line team, this is often best addressed by having a different telephone number for that service, so that the caller's first contact is again with a human.

Identification and Verification (ID&V)

Identification and verification (ID&V) can also be delivered via telephony, whereby the caller must, upon a pre-recorded voice prompt, provide an identifier, for example, a password stored on the telephony system, before being connected to the service they require.

As with IVR, automatic ID&V may be regarded as too impersonal for use in an HR SSC. There may also be concerns from a security standpoint about holding personal data on a telephony system. Moreover, it is in many cases inappropriate for callers to be required to have their identity verified if they are merely seeking some non-confidential, generic information such as a list of training courses or details of the organization's maternity policy.

Management Information (MI)

A contact centre telephony system will be able to record length of time per phone call so that performance against HR SSC service standards can be measured. For example, if calls handled by one agent are consistently longer than targeted levels, a training need will be highlighted.

Telephony MI can also be displayed on wallboards, showing statistics such as calls taken, waiting and lost, average pick-up times and so on, to provide a highly visual real-time snapshot of performance against the HR SSC's telephony service level agreements (SLAs).

Also, each telephone call can be recorded and stored, for example, for training purposes or to retain a permanent record of important conversations.

Integration with CRM

Standard interfaces have been developed between telephony and computer systems such as CRMs, using computer telephony integration (CTI) software. CTI offers a range of additional functionality, some of which may be applicable to HR SSCs. For example, if an HR SSC uses the telephony system's IVR and ID&V facilities, CTI can be used to further streamline the verification and routing processes as follows:

- the caller's identity can be verified by using a far wider range of data available from or via the CRM system; and

- while IVR is routing the caller to an appropriate agent, the CTI can open up the CRM at the relevant part of the customer's record, including full contact history, based on the type of service they have requested.

In summary, CTI offers the potential for further process efficiencies and savings in HR resource – in this case the call is handled by an appropriate agent who has all the relevant facts available before even speaking to the customer, who has already been verified. On the other hand, as stated above, this approach may be judged to be too blunt and impersonal an instrument for handling complex HR queries.

In this section we have looked at the different types of customer channel technologies, and how they can be integrated with the CRM. Let us now examine what happens within the CRM itself, to allow work to be allocated, processed and managed.

The Customer Relationship Management System (CRM)

The CRM in the HR SSC has a number of important functions:

- it provides a record of all customer contacts;

- it helps an HR SSC agent to clarify and answer a customer's query;

- it automates and streamlines the allocation and processing of cases, that is, work that results from a customer contact;

- it controls the throughput of work within the HR SSC;

- it provides management information to assist resource planning and management, and monitoring of the HR SSC's performance against its SLAs; and

- it delivers full HR SSC automation by integrating the contact channels (self-service, phone, paper and so on) with the back-office data processing applications such as HRIS/payroll.

These functions are described in more detail below.

RECORDING CONTACTS

As we have seen above, it is possible to configure the CRM to record details of all contacts. This allows a comprehensive contact history to be available to the agent when dealing with an employee. It also creates valuable MI, for example which types of query or which channels are generating the most usage.

ANSWERING QUERIES

One of the critical success factors of any HR SSC is that most calls can be responded to and closed by the agent on the spot, that is, without the need for any further work or having to contact the customer again.

In addition to their own knowledge, experience and training, the agents have access to various facilities provided by the CRM to help them handle the call:

- Contact history – all of the caller's previous contact details can be stored on the CRM to provide comprehensive background data, plus any relevant context, for example, via a screen pop-up to highlight that the caller is hard of hearing.

- Employee record – as stated above, a fully integrated CRM will be able to access the core HR/payroll system to display the employee's personnel record.

- Scripts – the CRM can prompt the agent to steer the conversation along a logical path to ensure that the query is clarified and answered accurately and comprehensively. For example, if employees within the same organization are entitled to different levels or types of benefit depending on qualifying criteria, a well-scripted CRM should prompt the agent to confirm with the customer which of the criteria are satisfied before answering the query.

- Knowledge management (KM) – a good CRM should offer a comprehensive electronic knowledge base, which can be populated with details of all HR policies, processes, procedures and terms and conditions. These documents may be stored in a variety of formats, for example, HTML, Microsoft Word or PDF files. They require initial indexing, for example, by title and/or keywords to allow easy retrieval by agents who may enter their query using their own words. The system then returns a list of possible entries, ordered by their contextual accuracy. When the agent selects the most appropriate entry, the KM system uses internal logic to strengthen the link between the wording of the original query and the selected answer. Thus the system 'learns' from usage to improve the accuracy of its responses. It is also able to develop a list of the most frequently asked questions (FAQs) on each topic, as a useful information tool for SSC agents and management. As with eDRMS systems, KM software may be supplied as part of the CRM or as a pre-integrated third party product. If neither case applies (for example, if the organization uses a different KM product), integration will be necessary.

On occasions where the agent is not able to answer the call, even with the knowledge base, they can either put the caller on hold and get advice from a second line specialist, or pass the caller (via a 'warm transfer') to that specialist, who will also have access to all of the above facilities.

If the query has been resolved during the call and no further work is needed, the CRM is used to log any important details of the call, which is categorized (for example, 'maternity query') for MI purposes.

ALLOCATING AND PROCESSING WORK

Many enquiries require further action before they can be closed, for example:

- a paper document being notified to the CRM by the eDRMS, following scanning and indexing; or

- a request by a line manager for the HR SSC to carry out a transaction, for example entering staff overtime details because the line manager does not have access to the necessary system.

In CRM parlance these are known as 'service requests' or 'cases' (though some CRMs reserve the word 'case' to describe a more complex, longer-running event, for example, a period of maternity leave or an employment tribunal).

The CRM may use 'workflow' technology to store the logic and rules involved in each HR process in order to orchestrate the execution of that process, for example, by sending an e-mail reminder to a line manager to take action because a task is now overdue, or prompting an appropriate HR agent to carry out a required task. Workflow technology is increasingly important in the delivery of the new HR service model, and the ability to automate process in this way is a key contributor to achieving efficiency savings in HR SSCs.

Service requests are managed as follows:

- they are first *classified* according to the process to which they relate (in more sophisticated systems, this classification will generate a set of tasks and associated due dates, according to the type of request);

- they are then *allocated* to (or picked up by) appropriate HR SSC agents;

  (the order of the above steps may vary depending upon the process in use within the HR SSC and the extent to which it is driven by classification)

- the required tasks within each case are then created (if they have not been automatically generated) and *executed*, prompted by workflow as described above;

- finally, when no more tasks are outstanding, the service request must be *closed*.

Classification

A request may be classified manually by an agent (or by the scanning team in the case of a paper document, as described earlier), or automatically, for example, via self-service depending upon the e-form used. This determines the basis on which the case will be allocated and executed.

Allocation

A service request may, depending on its classification, be allocated to a team of suitably qualified agents, one of whom will then adopt the request. Allocation can be automated by the CRM using data such as the request category and the agents' skill sets.

Execution

Each request may consist of a series of chronological or linked tasks – for example, a long-term absence may need following up at pre-defined points in the form of contacting the individual or requesting a medical report. These tasks will either have been generated automatically based on the classification or be created manually by the agent as the request is progressed. In highly automated solutions execution will be controlled by the workflow engine, which, at the appropriate point, will resurface the case to the relevant agent for action, or automatically generate and issue an e-mail or produce a letter.

Closure

When all tasks within the process have been successfully accomplished, the request can be closed by the agent, who will enter an appropriate reason for closure. The request will remain available for subsequent viewing until it is archived from the CRM system after an agreed period.

MANAGING WORK

Because all work in the HR SSC is tracked through the CRM, the system provides a continual snapshot of completed, outstanding or pending work. This can be used to monitor and reallocate workloads. For example, seriously out of date tasks can be pulled by supervisors from queues for immediate action, work can be re-allocated according to priorities and resource availability, training needs can be identified, for example if task execution times by agents are abnormally long. In short, in a fully automated HR SSC, every contact and transaction is logged on the system, so all work can be monitored and managed via the CRM. This is a radically different approach to the operation of the traditional HR office.

MANAGEMENT INFORMATION (MI)

The work management facilities described above are the most operational of several layers of management information available from the CRM system. Such operational data would typically be used to make hourly or daily management decisions, for example, work reallocation, resource redeployment and so on. As with telephony, appropriate data can be displayed on wallboards to provide a visible snapshot of KPIs, such as number of cases outstanding.

CRM data can also be extracted to generate a variety of higher level MI, for tactical and strategic HR management reporting. This is described in the HR MI section towards the end of this chapter.

FRONT TO BACK OFFICE INTEGRATION

We have examined how each of the customer contact channels such as paper, telephony, self-service and so on can be integrated with the CRM. Many of these transactions also require integration between the CRM and the back office applications such as the HRIS/payroll system, the learning management system and the resource management system.

By integrating the generic customer-facing office technology to the specialist back-end HR systems, and carrying out a range of processing using its own internal logic, the CRM binds together the fully automated HR SSC. As a result, a disparate set of systems and manual processes, with their inherent duplication and inefficiencies, are transformed into a streamlined and wholly integrated HR systems architecture.

To complete our review of HR SSC technology, let us now examine the specialist HR systems in the back-office.

HRIS/Payroll System and Specialist 'Add On' Packages

The two layers of back office HR technology – the HR/payroll system and specialist add-on software – are described together in this section. This is because in many products these two layers are designed to be fully integrated even though they may be purchased as separate modules.

The HRIS and payroll systems together form the core back-office technology. It is usually preferable for these two applications to be fully integrated within one product in order to avoid having to maintain duplicate data which has to be synchronized, often via a complex set of interfaces. However, there are cases where separation may be desirable or even a requirement, for example where the HR system is looked after by HR and the payroll system is run by the finance department, or sufficient investment is only available to purchase one or other module requiring deployment within a legacy system environment.

This core HR/payroll system will provide much of the functionality to support the major HR activities and processes, illustrated in the HR taxonomy of Figure 3.2.

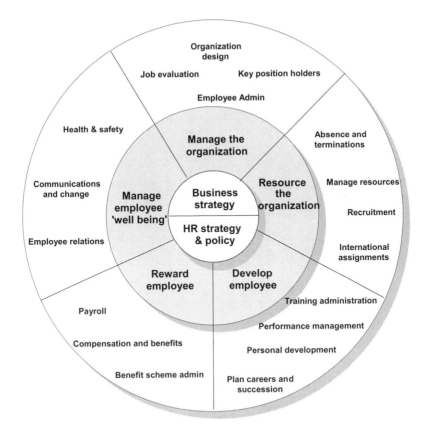

Figure 3.2   An integrated view of HR processes

HR packages provide different levels of coverage across these areas. Where coverage in a particular area is shallow, an organization may purchase add-on products to achieve the missing functionality. Although these products may be provided by other suppliers, a standard interface with the core HRIS may exist where the two suppliers have such an arrangement. Otherwise, new interfaces may need to be developed unless duplication is sufficiently limited so as not to merit this.

The principal applications provided by HR back-office technology products are described below.

HR ADMINISTRATION

This covers the core HR processes – starters, leavers, transfers, absence, overtime and so on – which have traditionally been the preserve of the HRIS. However, until recently at least, the HRIS has often been little more than a data repository, as a result of which the core HR processes have had to be carried out manually by HR administrators. With modern web-enabled workflow-driven HR systems, however, these processes can be highly streamlined so that task owners (employees, line managers, HR staff) are prompted automatically to execute their tasks using employee or manager self-service (ESS/MSS).

As an example of the above, an employee may submit a request for annual leave, which is routed through to their manager to authorize. The system prompts the manager that the employee has submitted the leave request, and does so again if there is no response within a prescribed period. When the manager accesses the request, the system provides a summary of that unit's known absence for the period concerned to help reach a decision. When a decision is entered, the system is updated as appropriate and a note of the decision routed to the employee.

All of the above types of procedure are governed by user-programmable logic built into the system's workflow engine. As noted earlier, workflow functionality is also provided by CRM systems or generic third-party automation tools, so an evaluation of IT architectural options is important when workflow engines are being considered.

Various add-ons may be used to supplement the HR administration component of the core system. For example, in a clocking-on environment, a separate time and attendance system may be used to record absence details, which are then passed to the HRIS via an interface. The HR IS may also need to integrate with systems that are external to the HR department, such as security, accommodation, expenses and so on.

REWARD

Payroll

The payroll system is perhaps the most established among back-office HR systems. Because payroll system requirements are so well understood by payroll practitioners it is not proposed to describe them in any detail here, and a summary of key functional requirements should suffice. However, this should not obscure the fact that, despite the ever-increasing sophistication of HR technology, payroll remains the one component above all others that must work correctly.

The main functions of payroll software are as follows:

- permitting the entry of all payments and deductions;

- calculating gross and net pay;

- generating payments via BACS, by cheque or manually;

- generating payslips;

- payroll reporting;

- payroll accounting and integration with the finance system;

- processing of weekly and monthly staff payrolls;

- allowing supplementary payments, after the main payroll run;

- year-end procedures, reporting, data transfer and so on;

- processing pensioners' payrolls;

- processing offshore payrolls (Isle of Man, Channel Islands and so on);

- processing expatriate payments;

- interfacing with internal and external benefits providers, including pensions.

As stated earlier, unless organizational constraints dictate otherwise, it is desirable for the payroll system to be integrated with the core HR system, since there is considerable overlap of data and process.

Compensation Administration

The system should allow pay increases to be modeled according to pre-defined rules. For example, in a performance-related pay system, there may be a total pay increase budget, including on-costs (employer pension and NI contributions) which is required to be distributed within pre-determined ranges according to performance ratings. The system should allow a departmental manager to model various scenarios in order to determine the preferred distribution, and then submit this to the authorizing manager for sign-off and implementation.

A similar approach may be taken to other compensation applications such as the planning and delivery of executive share awards and sales staff bonuses. If this functionality is not supported within the core HRIS/payroll, additional tools such as spreadsheets will be required, including a two-way interface to supply the existing data to the spreadsheet and accept the agreed awards for implementation.

Benefits Administration

A range of benefits may be catered for by HR systems or additional tools on top, for example private medical cover, company cars, share option schemes, Give as You Earn and so on. The most basic requirement is to make payroll deductions and generate lists of scheme participants. If additional data, for example membership details and scheme rules, are needed, these may either reside on the HRIS's benefits module if it has one, or on a separate system. In the latter case an interface will be needed between the HRIS and the relevant benefits system. This may be achieved by a traditional batch interface planned around the payroll run, or by a web services interface if real-time access to scheme details is required with sufficient regularity throughout the pay cycle.

Pensions schemes are massively more complex than other types of benefits and are usually administered via specialist software, although some HR system suppliers do include pensions modules within their core offering. If the pensions operation is within the scope of the HR SSC, a web services interface between the pensions system and the CRM may be worth exploring. This may be useful even if all pensions queries are routed straight through to the second line pensions experts, in order to manage pensions workloads and generate MI via the CRM.

Note that the purpose of a pensions administration system is to manage membership, contributions and accrual details for employees and deferred pensioners. Payment of pensioners who are in receipt of their pension is usually processed via the main payroll system. Various interfaces between the HRIS/payroll system and the pensions administration system are therefore usually needed.

Finally, the HRIS and/or add-on package may be used to administer flexible benefits schemes, whereby salary is sacrificed in order to purchase a range of employee-related products and services, for example, the purchase of additional holiday or a private health insurance plan.

ORGANIZATION MANAGEMENT (OM)

Organization management (OM) is now a standard offering of HR products and provides a record of the organization, which is separate from the individuals who populate it. OM allows the organization to be represented in terms of departments and/or functions, spanning as many organizational layers as required. Within these, reporting hierarchies are recorded comprising individual positions, which may be vacant or occupied by one or more employees whose records are linked to OM from the HR administration module.

Generic jobs can also be recorded, for example, 'HR business partner', to which attributes, for example, competencies, training requirements and so on can be assigned. Positions may be allocated to jobs and 'inherit' these attributes, if required.

OM enhances HR functionality across a range of applications:

- *Resourcing* – where position attributes can be used to create vacancy records, when the incumbent is shown as leaving (see below);

- *Learning and development* – where competency matching between individuals and their current or intended positions can be conducted for development planning purposes (see below);

- *Management information* – providing analyses of filled and vacant positions, job competency profiles and so on. The OM module may also generate organization charts showing filled and vacant positions, although a specialist charting package is often needed as an add-on to achieve a sufficiently user-friendly display;

- *System security* – OM hierarchies may be used to control access rights among ESS/MSS users based on hierarchies, for example, a line manager can only access the records of staff occupying positions in his or her department;

- *Workflow* rules may well be governed by OM; for example, determining where to route a request for annual leave. As mentioned previously, the workflow may reside in the CRM layer, in which case an interface with OM data would be needed to supply the CRM with the necessary hierarchy details;

- *Payroll charging* – rather than maintaining cost centre details individually for every employee in a department, it is more efficient to record the cost centre once, on OM against the department. Employees will then inherit the cost centre details via their positions, and only in exceptional cases would these need to be overwritten by individual level cost centre entries. Apart from economy of data entry, this improves accuracy and consistency between the HR and finance systems.

In summary, OM supports a range of critical HR functions and as such is the backbone of the HRIS and related systems. It is therefore essential that OM data is accurate and up to date, requiring robust data maintenance procedures.

RESOURCING

The following web-enabled functionality is normally available within the HRIS or specialist recruitment administration system (RMS):

- creating a vacancy, usually by transferring job data from the OM module upon a position being shown as vacant, or potentially vacant;

- advertising the vacancy on the company's intranet or external web site, or via third-party recruitment sites;

- recording and administering applications;

- managing the selection process, using workflows to route actions between managers, applicants and HR staff;

- administering medicals, references and contracts for preferred candidates;

- completing the employment of the successful individuals by transferring their details onto the HR administration module via the starter process;

- generating MI, for example, interview schedules, lists of positions currently being advertised and so on.

Other more specialist resourcing applications may be provided as part of the RMS or via third-party software, for example, CV scanning and analysis and on-line psychometric testing. If a separate RMS is deployed, interfaces with the core HRIS may be needed, and also with the CRM if this is used to front-end resourcing for work control and MI purposes.

LEARNING AND DEVELOPMENT

Learning management system (LMS) software is normally available within HR packages or can be purchased separately, requiring integration with the core system. Web-based LMSs can be used by managers, employees and training staff to plan and administer all types of learning intervention, for example, courses, e-learning and coaching. Typically such systems will hold a range of data:

- a catalogue of learning options, pre-requisites and course dates;

- a learning resource inventory;

- a record of learning expenses incurred;

- competency/learning requirements associated with positions/jobs (from the OM module), against which employees' competency attainments may be profiled;

- employee learning data (learning plan, training history, competencies, qualifications and so on) from the personnel administration database.

LMSs are particularly useful where the acquisition of qualifications is mandatory, for example, in a regulatory environment.

E-learning can be launched from many LMSs, and the results stored automatically upon completion of modules or the entire course. This requires integration between the LMS and the e-learning system, and various industry interface standards are now available to facilitate this. Some LMSs contain authoring tools for creating e-learning content, and this type of more comprehensive package is known as an integrated learning system (ILS).

Performance management also lends itself to web-based HR systems or specialist add-ons, allowing the recording and monitoring of objectives, training plans, logs and appraisals.

Specialist succession planning software can also be used to record who are earmarked for which jobs, and what development they will require before succeeding to them. These results can be displayed graphically to provide a highly visual view of the succession plan, highlighting where key gaps may exist.

Learning and development (L&D) systems must also be able to produce basic operational MI, for example, course attendees, plus a range of tactical and strategic MI (see next section).

MANAGEMENT INFORMATION (MI)

HR MI can be viewed as one of three types:

Operational MI

Operational MI refers to the day-to-day requirements for information to support ongoing operational processes. This has already been dealt with when describing individual systems, for example, calls lost (telephony), cases awaiting attention (CRM), course attendee lists (HRIS or LMS) and interview schedules (HRIS or RMS).

Tactical MI

The purpose of tactical MI is to help determine and measure HR performance and the effectiveness of HR policies. Examples might include:

- measurement of key performance indicators in HR;

- comparing absence or other workforce statistics across departments;

- analysing learning plans to identify where corporate learning initiatives might be needed;

- comparing the effectiveness of advertising media;

- analysing salary distributions for performance related pay (PRP) management purposes;

- measuring performance against diversity targets;

- aggregating operational CRM and telephony data to assess the HR SSC's performance against SLAs.

Whilst this type of information may not be required instantly, it is likely to be needed consistently, that is, to regular schedules and in agreed formats, but also allowing further manipulation by users, for example, standard on-line reports for line managers configured for use in the day-to-day management of their particular part of the business.

Strategic MI

Strategic HR MI is perhaps best exemplified by the balanced scorecard approach, which is used to supply senior management with a snapshot view of a defined set of business-critical indicators. Problem areas or hotspots can be highlighted to executives by means of simple 'traffic light' mechanisms so that executive time can be focused on addressing key issues.

A further requirement might be to be able to spot trends that may lie outside the parameters set by strategic plans in order to highlight other critical issues that might otherwise have escaped senior management attention. An example of this might be where the CRM reports a sudden upsurge in pension queries, which might result from press coverage of pension scheme deficits. In this case the system has acted as the organization's 'ear to the ground', perhaps prompting the issue of a reassuring pensions bulletin to help avert a potentially serious staffing issue.

HR MI and the HR SSC

HR SSC management and specialists are likely to be the major users of operational MI, most of which supports HR administration and the day-to-day running of the HR SSC. Most tactical MI and virtually all strategic MI is more likely to be used outside the HR SSC, for example, by HR business partners, line managers and corporate executives. However, it is the HR SSC's job to ensure that on-line MI is available to users, and as such the HR SSC is the owner of all HR MI facilities.

HR MI Technology

From a systems perspective, HR MI has traditionally been the preserve of the HRIS and, by definition, its main purpose. This has now changed because of:

- the emergence of the HR CRM and associated front office technology, which has made available new types of HR MI; and

- the advent of advanced 'analytic' or 'data warehouse' software into which data from various systems can be extracted and manipulated extensively.

As a consequence, HR MI is increasingly seen as spanning all of the technology layers.

FRONT-OFFICE SYSTEMS MI

As seen above, systems such as telephony and the CRM are capable of delivering their own operational MI, which can be summarized and aggregated to provide tactical and occasionally strategic MI. The MI generated can also be used for HR SSC financial management. For example, if it transpires that a disproportionate amount of agent time was spent dealing with service requests in a particular department, that department can be billed accordingly or its budget revised for next year.

BACK-OFFICE SYSTEMS MI

As the name suggests, the HRIS should offer sophisticated MI facilities, perhaps comprising a range of configurable standard reports plus ad hoc query and reporting tools. These facilities should be easy to use and distributable electronically, for access by line managers and HR business partners throughout the organization via web browsers.

The standard reports should cover requirements such as headcount, absence and turnover statistics, which are common but complex to program. For example, absence statistics need to aggregate all working days lost, by reason, and present them as a percentage of working days available. The output must be capable of being configured by users in order to analyse it, for example, by period, department, age group, grade, gender or absence types.

The query tools should flexibly deliver both *statistics*, for example, numbers of staff qualifying for a certain benefit, analysed by grade; and *lists*, for example, of the staff concerned sorted alphabetically within department.

Any tools on top are likely to contain their own reporting facilities. Indeed, some of them, for example, organization charting and succession planning packages, may have been purchased precisely because they are capable of manipulating and presenting data in complex or graphical ways.

INTEGRATED MI

HR MI used for tactical and strategic purposes is usually extracted into a separate third-party reporting system, often referred to as an 'analytics' package or 'data warehouse'. This has several advantages as set out below:

- *Combining different types of HR data*: In order to provide holistic HR MI, it may be necessary to combine organizational staffing information, for example corporate absence statistics, with HR functional performance data like compliance with SSC SLAs. These can only be provided in a consistent format if they are produced from the same database, rather than from separate systems where the source data may be inconsistent due to errors, or extracted over different periods and populations.

- *Combining HR and non-HR data*: It may also be necessary to combine HR with other functional data, for example finance data for corporate reporting purposes. One example might be comparing the performance of HR and IT SSCs against organization-wide customer service SLAs. Another might be the production of cross-functional balanced scorecard statistics.

- *Consistency*: Extracted rather than real-time data is usually desirable for non-operational MI purposes. This is because a suite of reports run from a real-time system will yield inconsistent results since the source data will be constantly changing. Static datasets created to an agreed schedule are needed, which can be aggregated over time to support tactical and strategic MI reporting, using snapshot and trend data.

- *Functionality*: Specialist analytics software is likely to be more powerful than the MI facilities of HR packages because it has been designed with the sole purpose of complex data manipulation and presentation. This will include, for example, the ability to 'slice and dice' data by any variable and present the resultant information in a range of flexible and graphical reporting formats.

- *System performance*: Strategic reports are likely to involve data compiled over lengthy periods, for example, comparisons of absence data between the current and previous years. In HR systems, which are designed for transactional processing, it is necessary to archive historical data after an agreed period in order to conserve disk space and preserve response times, which can also be adversely affected by running reports in the live system. Specialist analytics systems, on the other hand, are designed to hold specific data in a condensed format in a dedicated reporting environment, allowing a far greater range of historical reporting without affecting response times in the live system.

- *IT strategy*: the IT strategy in many organizations limits aggregate reporting across all functions and departments to one common analytics package. This maximizes flexibility by standardizing user reporting skills throughout the organization, whilst minimizing IT support requirements. The downside is that its features may not be equally suited to each department's needs, resulting in a lack of functionality in some cases.

In summary, a variety of reasons exist for aggregating HR data into a dedicated analytics package, leaving the systems from which the data are sourced to be used for mainly operational reporting purposes. Once again, the solution involves some degree of systems integration, which is the subject of the next section.

The Integration Argument

There has been a continuous debate in IT circles as to whether, taken together, business and technology needs are best served by a single integrated HR technology solution from one supplier covering a broad range of functionality, or a number of specialist packages sitting on top of a core database, that is, a 'best of breed' solution, requiring a variety of interfaces to pass data between the various systems.

We have encountered the integration issue at virtually every stage of our journey round the HR SSC technology landscape, for example, whether the CRM should have in-built e-DRMS or KM systems, whether the HRIS and payroll functionality should come as one integrated product, whether add-ons should be used for specialist HR applications, for example, LMS, and to what extent an integrated MI database is needed for tactical and strategic reporting purposes. Let us now consider some of the key arguments in the single supplier versus best of breed debate.

SINGLE SUPPLIER APPROACH

The single integrated solution is preferred by IT managers because:

- it is easier to receive external support in that all service requests are handled by the same supplier, so that problems can never fall between two stools;

- the IT department can deliver more cost-effective internal support because the skills are more interchangeable between applications; and

- perhaps most significantly, there are fewer interfaces to develop, support and maintain.

In the case of HR, it is perfectly feasible for one supplier to provide most if not all components of the systems landscape. For example, enterprise resource planning (ERP) suppliers like Oracle and SAP offer both a CRM and an integrated HRIS/payroll module which includes most of the specialist add-on functionality that we have encountered. For good measure these providers also offer a range of other functional applications (most notably finance from our standpoint), as well as common or 'open' development environments, which purport to offer maximal ease of integration with other suppliers' products.

From a business perspective, the advantages in this approach of getting cost-effective IT support are often outweighed by:

- a perceived lack of choice imposed by the IT department ('you can have any colour you want as long as it's black'); and

- an often justified belief that the needs of individual HR teams, for example, learning, reward and so on are compromised by the functional limitations of some aspects of the generic solution.

It is also important to explore the extent to which different components within the single supplier solution are truly integrated. For example, whilst a supplier may offer both an HRIS/payroll solution and a CRM, it is possible that these two components have never previously been combined or indeed were not even designed with this combination in mind (not impossible given the relatively recent adoption of CRM for HR purposes). In this case, the implementation cost and risk may be increased by the need for the development of 'invisible interfaces' by the supplier.

In summary, the single integrated solution is fine in principle, and totally sensible from an IT standpoint, but can involve perceived and often genuine disadvantages for HR that must be properly evaluated on a truly informed basis in order to avoid recriminations at a later stage.

BEST-OF-BREED APPROACH

The 'best of breed' model is generally unattractive to the IT department because of the costs associated with the additional internal and external support effort required, and the need to create, support and maintain numerous interfaces between disparate packages. Any two applications not explicitly designed to share data and work in an integrated manner will require some form of bespoke interface. Such interfaces are often highly complex and expensive to build and create a potential point of failure in the system. This requires comprehensive and detailed error-handling procedures, for example when inputting absence data into the HRIS/payroll system via the CRM.

From HR's standpoint, on the other hand, the individual packages may have the advantage of satisfying all rather than most of their functional needs. For example, a dedicated learning management solution from a specialist supplier may deliver more comprehensive functionality than the training module of an integrated system. Furthermore, some single supplier solutions simply do not offer certain types of functionality at all, for example, succession planning, whilst in other cases, their offering is so manifestly poor (organization charts being an oft-cited example) that the need to purchase add-ons becomes unavoidable. The argument is further complicated by HR functions determined to buy solutions with the widest range of functionality rather than making sure that there has been a thorough examination of what the business actually needs. Failure to do this will result in a poor investment decision undermining HR's drive towards establishing its commercial credentials with the business.

A further complicating factor is how each system is accessed and used. For example, if staff and managers are required to use self-service facilities within a number of different HR packages, for example HR administration, LMS, RMS and so on, they may need to learn each product's basic functions, such as system navigation and the use of special function keys. They may even have to remember a set of different user IDs and passwords, though this can be mitigated if each system complies with standards allowing 'single sign-on' (additional cost to the business case if not already available) whereby the required level of access to all appropriate systems is controlled at a higher 'portal' level when users first sign on to their organization's IT network.

In summary, the use of some best of breed solutions is often desirable, and occasionally inevitable, but this approach may involve considerable additional complexity, cost and risk. At the same time, the importance of understanding the requirements of end users is critical to the success of the transformation process itself. The ease with which the new service is adopted by users is the acid test when determining whether the design is right, for applications which users cannot adapt to quickly will cause service levels to fall, undermining HR's credibility.

SINGLE SUPPLIER VERSUS BEST OF BREED – SOME CONCLUSIONS

Many organizations have found that their 'best of breed' strategy has not delivered the promised vision of providing the best available functionality as a result of problems with integrating different products. Organizations that have pursued this route have often found that the potential advantage of superior functionality is quickly wiped out by a system with unreliable interfaces that does not adequately support the end-to-end process and relies on data held in different locations.

On the other hand, monolithic ERP-style solutions do not come cheap, may fail to supply the required level of functionality in all areas, and may even fail to deliver full integration benefits because not all components of their solution are truly integrated.

If this were not complicated enough, the HR technology scenario continues to evolve, and further factors have come into play during recent years:

- The use of CRM in HR SSCs offers a major integrating opportunity by linking the generic customer channel technology such as telephony and document imaging to the back-office HR applications. On the other hand, as we have seen, it introduces yet more requirements for interfaces and permutations for deploying workflow and self-service within the total systems architecture.

- The advent of web services integration allows real-time interfacing between web-enabled systems. In the case of view-only integration at least, this eliminates much of the complexity that existed in building interfaces between systems. Moreover, new standards for developing IT applications including interfaces are emerging, collectively known as 'service-oriented architecture' (SOA). As its name suggests, SOA is focused upon delivering IT solutions based on the quality of service they offer rather than being constrained by 'technocentric' factors. As SOA matures and is adopted by the major suppliers, it will further reduce the complexity involved in integrating different products.

In short, the integration issue is highly complex and far-reaching, and needs to be worked through by all interested parties, taking account of a wide range of factors which will vary between organizations. As a general rule, however, we would recommend a strategy of using a single integrated HR and payroll solution, probably from a single supplier, as a starting point. Any additional packages should be evaluated carefully in terms of the benefits they offer versus the cost, complexity and risk they create, focusing on what is truly essential rather than on what is nice to have. Organizations should investigate thoroughly the 'true cost of ownership' of the alternative technology landscapes, that is, the cost of implementing, running and supporting each solution, including all interfaces. The techniques involved in creating a business case and selecting a solution are explored further in subsequent chapters.

Security and Controls

Given the confidential nature of HR data, it is evident that effective security is a major requirement of HR SSC technology, which must support the organization's compliance with data protection principles:

- only relevant data are captured;

- data are accurately maintained;

- data are retained for no longer than necessary;

- data are used for legitimate purposes;

- access to data is controlled;

- data are disposed of safely.

FUNCTIONALITY

The features required to help achieve compliance with the data protection principles listed above are as follows:

Only Relevant Data are Captured

By controlling the capture of data within legitimate HR processes, the technology can be used to ensure that only relevant data are captured. Branches can be applied within the processing logic to further refine this. For example, if an employee is not entitled to a particular benefit, meaning that certain data items should not be recorded in their case, HR systems can be configured to prevent such input.

Data are Accurately Maintained

Various facilities exist to help keep data up to date and accurate:

- validation rules can be applied to input screens to prevent inaccurate data entry;

- self-service can be used by employees and managers to inspect and where appropriate change data;

- audit reports are available to provide a record of what has been changed;

- reports can be run for data verification purposes, for example the Freedom of Information Act.

Data are Retained for No Longer than Necessary

By means of processes or reports, HR systems are able to highlight data which are about to become too old to be retained, so that a decision can be made as to whether they should be deleted or archived off the database.

Data are Used for Legitimate Purposes

Again, by controlling the capture of data within specified HR processes, the technology can be used to ensure that data are only used for legitimate purposes.

Access to Data is Controlled

Various features are available to ensure that system access is confined to authorized users, and that the nature of their access is appropriate:

- as described earlier, telephony and CRM systems support ID&V, to prevent unauthorized callers gaining access to personal HR data;

- this can be extended to ensure that authorized callers only get access to data to which they are entitled. For example, OM can be used by the agent to confirm that the manager on the phone is responsible for the employee who is the subject of their call;

- HR systems offer secure ID and password logon facilities. As mentioned earlier, if multiple systems are in use, they should comply with generic access standards so that appropriate access across all systems is granted to users via a single sign-on;

- stringent technical security provisions can be applied, for example, encryption of passwords, secure web data transfer protocols (HTTPS) and so on;

- powerful security management facilities should be available for use by system administrators, for example, password resets, setting up and changing user groups and so on;

- access within systems should be confined to appropriate transactions (for example, being able to update all new starter details except payroll) and data (for example, managers are only given access to their own staff's data);

- the audit log will show which user carried out each data update.

DATA ARE DISPOSED OF SAFELY

HR systems should offer effective data archiving facilities so that, after an agreed period (and perhaps prompted by the system as mentioned above), data can be archived into secure off-line storage or deleted with absolute certainty.

SECURITY AND CONTROLS SUMMARY

As might be expected from the confidential nature of the HR SSC's work, HR technology has been developed to support comprehensive security requirements. Once again the implications of integration should not be overlooked – the higher the number of systems that are in use, the greater the effort (and cost) that is needed to ensure that all are configured in a consistent manner to ensure that the above requirements are satisfied across all HR SSC systems.

SUMMARY OF CHAPTER MESSAGES

- To deliver excellent customer service, the HR SSC is organized into a front and back office, each of which is supported by a range of technology.

- The front office technology comprises two integrated layers – customer channel technology (for example, telephony, self-service, document imaging) and the customer relationship management system (CRM).

- The back office technology also comprises two integrated layers – the core HRIS/payroll system and specialist add-on packages (also known as 'tools on top'). These span the full range of HR applications – HR administration, reward management, organization management, resourcing and learning and development.

- The front and back office technology components are also integrated with each other, resulting in a comprehensive and fully automated HR SSC. This is orchestrated by the CRM system, which services all HR contacts, queries and transactions, and is thus able to control the allocation and throughput of the HR SSC's entire workload.

- All operational and some tactical HR management information (MI) is delivered by individual systems, for example, telephony, CRM and HRIS/payroll. Other tactical and all strategic MI are provided by a separate, dedicated reporting (or 'analytics') package into which data are extracted and integrated from all HR technology layers.

- Effective systems integration is vital to the successful deployment of HR SSC technology. As a starting point, a strategy based on a single integrated product should be considered, with additional packages evaluated according to the benefits they offer versus their cost, including that of developing, supporting and maintaining interfaces.

- Appropriate security and control mechanisms are available within each layer of HR technology, and should be deployed rigorously and consistently to ensure compliance with data protection principles.

PART III

Managing the Transition

Linking Strategy to Technology

In previous chapters we have seen how the HR function has evolved from its traditional roots, typified as reactive, lacking commercial credentials and administratively inefficient, to being a prominent player in the reengineering of the 'administrative back office'. David Ulrich (see Chapter 1) provided the academic backbone, illustrating how a step change in operational performance could be achieved through the development of the shared service model, with Business Partners providing the long sought after strategic advantage through better alignment of HR and the business agenda.

However, it is now over ten years since Ulrich first proposed the new model for HR, and whilst the differentiation of transactional, change agent and expert roles has driven many success stories, there have been an equal number of attempts to implement the model that have not produced results, have caused cost overruns and may even have had a negative impact on the service they were supposed to be improving.

In the same period, the history of HR technology is littered with examples of HR systems that failed to deliver the promised performance and made no discernable impact on the strategic direction of the organization.

With a decade of hindsight to draw on, what are the differentiating factors that separate the successful HR strategies from the failures, and why is it that programmes that are similarly resourced, funded and managed can have radically different results? How does the execution of the HR strategy impact and influence the design of the technology that serves it, and how can the organization ensure that the complex process of delivering an HR transformation technology architecture remains anchored in the strategic imperatives of the HR function and the business as a whole?

In this part of the book we examine the process of technology delivery and how the common pitfalls can be avoided. As a starting point for the journey this chapter explores how the planning and design of a technical solution for HR can be harnessed to the business and HR strategic planning process to ensure the development of cost-effective and impactful systems that truly support the transformational model.

What Fire are You Trying to Put Out?

Whilst there may be differences of emphasis, the drivers behind the delivery of the new HR model tend to be common. Specifically, the grail pursued by most organizations is to improve the quality of service provided by HR, whilst at the same time providing measurable improvements in performance and reducing operational costs.

It is typically at this point that transformation programmes in HR will start to diverge. In our experience, organizations will, too often, focus the majority of effort and attention on those areas that have historically been seen as key in any change programme:

- detailed process mapping and redesign;

- in depth reviews of technical requirements and evaluation of software solutions;

- the logistics of setting up a shared service centre.

Whilst these areas are important, there is a danger that, in focusing on these issues alone, the programme will fall into the trap of losing sight of the whole HR delivery model and how the service centre and the HR system will support the overall model. More significantly, the level of detail demanded by these tasks can lead many programmes to lose touch with the demands and requirements of the business and the way in which HR can most effectively support it.

Our own experience and analysis of successful and unsuccessful shared services projects highlights five key criteria for success. Specifically organizations should expressly consider how to:

- define the service the business actually needs;

- ensure the design for the HR service model is fully integrated with the way in which the business operates;

- manage a process that acknowledges the natural business resistance to the change and the time it takes to embed it;

- establish post-implementation disciplines to ensure that HR is run in a commercial and business-like fashion;

- make intelligent use of technology that is closely integrated to the HR strategy and the main drivers of the business.

Once these questions are understood and planned for, then the organization will be in a position to plan for the intelligent use of technology; one that supports the principal objectives of the change whilst ensuring that systems are delivered in a cost-effective manner.

Service-Led Design – A Service the Business Needs

Recent research conducted by Personnel Today identified that 60 per cent of HR professionals believed their function to be effective whilst only 20 per cent of their senior colleagues in other functions agreed with that view. Clearly HR is fundamentally failing to show that it can deliver a service that provides real value in most organizations.

The pressure is on HR to demonstrate that, whatever aspects of the new model are being introduced to the organization, such as shared services or business partnering, then both sides must have a clear understanding of exactly what they want from the service and be clear about how the new model will change and improve current operations. Failure to do this will result in a solution that will not be perceived as valuable by the business and will reinforce the perception that HR is ineffective.

This inevitably means starting the design process at the top of the organization and agreeing with key business stakeholders what features of the HR service will really make a difference to how their business is supported. Early investigation and analysis of these top level requirements with the senior team in the organization will form the core design principles that provide the anchor for how the whole solution will be designed, developed and installed within the organization.

There may be the temptation with the development of a new HR service model to carry out an in-depth review of current and future process models. However, the discipline of starting with service requirements provides the basis to shape, design and deliver a solution the business will actually use rather than one that just meets the needs of HR.

A well-articulated set of design principles will form the touchstone for the service design to which the programme team can return to keep them honest in the complexities of running the change programme. In addition, the process of involving senior layers of the organization in the design process will help foster an environment for change that will permeate all layers in the business and greatly simplify the messages that need to be developed in detail at a later stage.

If the design principles are clear from the outset, organizations will avoid one of the most common causes of failure, namely a disconnect between the objectives of the business and the tactical delivery plans put in place by HR.

Avoiding Fragmentation – Integrating the HR Model

The principles laid out by David Ulrich and embodied in the design of many HR organizations are typically composed of three parts:

- the operational 'delivery engine' – frequently defined as the shared services function;

- the overall strategic corporate direction or policy in the business – often described as 'centres of excellence' or 'centres of expertise' (CofEs);

- the specific demands of the business and those represented within it – often embodied in the role of the HR business partner (HR BP).

A key part of making the HR model work involves establishing the activities and accountabilities of the main protagonists to ensure the organization realizes maximum economies of scale and skill.

The change programme brings significant challenges at all levels: the setting up of a shared service operation demands a major re-evaluation of the HR function, reorganization of the core processes on a grand scale and selling the concept and the revised model to an often sceptical organization. At the same time, a newly enfranchised business partner may find that the struggle to establish credibility and definition in this new role is undermined by teething difficulties experienced in the service centre.

Whilst much has been written about the responsibilities of these discrete roles, the overall design of the HR service is often left incomplete by a failure to establish how the independent roles will work as part of an integrated whole. Too often we meet organizations where the different parts of the HR organization work against one another and fail to realize the objective of delivering an integrated service to the business.

The problem can be exacerbated (see Figure 4.1) when the relationships with the service users or clients are considered in relation to HR. Any breakdown in the relationship between the shared service centre (SSC) and the client (for example through transition problems or service delivery failures) will inevitably affect the relationship between the HR BP and the client, usually resulting in the HR BP being told to 'go away and fix it' before any strategic level discussions can take place.

Similarly, any failure on the part of the business partner to understand the business need and build this into effective demand plans will frustrate the service centre's ability to deliver. The result is often an HR service that is fragmented and disconnected in the eyes of the customer.

Such shortcomings and failures are commonplace during the complex transition phase and often stretch the concept of a single integrated HR function (sometimes referred to as 'one HR') to breaking point. Not surprisingly, alienation between the component roles in HR will only underline the business view that 'HR isn't working'.

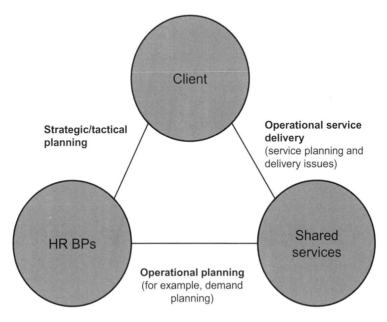

Figure 4.1 Relationships in the new HR model

Against this backdrop it is essential that the HR function in transition is able to develop a 'one HR' mentality and demonstrate a level of integration that operates on a number of levels:

- *operationally*: by means of common processes that apply equally to the shared service centre, the business partners and the centres of expertise;

- *intellectually*: through effective sharing of knowledge and provision of access to core HR data;

- *socially*: through the development of a 'one HR' identity;

- *emotionally*: through shared values and sense of purpose;

- *technologically*: through a common toolset and source of data.

Managing Change – Anticipating Resistance

The cost benefits of the transformation process can be significant and can undermine the integrity of the change process by dominating and dictating the pace of change. The cost benefits arising from, say, the implementation of a shared services model should be the positive outcome of a change programme whose primary aim is to ensure absolute best practice in the function.

A programme focused purely on cost savings is likely to 'undershoot' and miss critical benefits in terms of performance and service improvements. All parts of the business from the top down must engage with the change programme from day one and understand what HR is striving to achieve. Involvement of the line management, users and customers of HR is essential to build a business-focused delivery programme.

Our own examination of successful change programmes in HR reveals common success factors:

- *Build early commitment*: Change of this magnitude is rarely welcomed by everyone with open arms; there may be a very natural business resistance to losing the intimacy of a locally based HR service in favour of, say, a shared service centre. The fact that many shared service centres experience teething problems well into the first 12 months of operation may exacerbate this resistance unless the commitment to the change is built early and at a senior level and unless common misconceptions about HR and the service are addressed.

- *Focus on the basics*: Service success comes from a service designed with the needs of all key users in mind. This may mean taking account of seemingly mundane requirements for basic operational improvements. However, buy-in from key stakeholders will only be forthcoming if the HR model is seen to be addressing existing issues and not just those that might be exciting future developments in the function.

- *Manage expectations*: As discussed, transformation on any scale will inevitably take time and it is rare for all component parts of the model to work effectively from day one. Our experience shows that services can deteriorate in the early stages before they improve and audiences must be primed for this eventuality. Overselling what is achievable at the outset will inevitably lead to disappointment and disillusionment with the transformation process and undermine the credibility of the service. Again the key is to manage expectations about the pace of change and likely outcomes with key internal audiences to ensure that realistic and demonstrable timelines are mutually acceptable. Agree it, document it and constantly review it!

- *Seek specialist support*: Change programmes are, by definition, the antithesis of business-as-usual and, as such, demand specialized skills not found in abundance in most organizations. Working with external advisers may or may not be part of the experience and culture of the organization, but establishing a team that can demonstrate deep understanding of the issues is essential. A proven track record in the delivery team is an essential pre-requisite.

MANAGING HR LIKE A BUSINESS

Whilst the effectiveness of the new model is heavily dependent on the transition process, long-term delivery of results will be dependent on post-implementation success and the ability of the new HR service to develop and manage a new set of operational disciplines.

Specifically, HR will need to understand its client businesses and anticipate their needs; it will need rigorous focus on process improvement and it will require management of a slick back-office function that does not intrude on the deployment of the strategic service. In short, HR needs to develop commercial management disciplines that allow HR to be run on business lines.

In practical terms, this means HR must develop a focus on four key areas:

- *Service management*: Developing the ability to define, measure and track performance levels in the organization. The ability to demonstrate progress and improvement over time is a key factor in determining the overall success of the change programme as well as providing an historical basis to track the peaks and troughs in demand for services.

- *Customer management*: The new model must allow for a customer voice to be heard in decisions about the management of the service. This will ensure that the good work done in the design phase to build relevant services will be carried through into the long term. The roles of the business partner, service centre account managers and the line manager are all critical to ensure that HR provides a dynamic service that flexes readily to the needs of the business.

- *Performance improvement*: Long-term performance in HR will be driven by continuous improvement which, in turn, demands accurate performance data and the clear identification of the opportunities to re-engineer processes. Methods such as Six Sigma may help to drive this process, but it fundamentally requires a will and a capability in the HR management team.

- *Financial management*: Pricing of transactional services in HR may be aspirational at the outset of a transformation programme but may become a possibility and a requirement as the model reaches maturity. The ability to understand the detailed cost elements of HR and their underlying drivers is critical to ongoing development of the service and is dependent in turn on the quality of management information systems.

These disciplines are often seen as unnecessary luxuries in terms of capability and resource. Whilst they may be in place during the implementation phase, they may then be wound down once the service has gone live. In our experience, service launch is the real start of the transformation journey and it is from this point that these key business functions can be even more critical.

INTELLIGENT USE OF TECHNOLOGY

Where then does this leave the plan for building an integrated technology platform and, in the midst of such complex change? How can the practitioner ensure that the technology infrastructure is closely aligned with the objectives of the programme, the HR function and the aspirations of the business as a whole?

An examination of the statistics around technology delivery may be a useful starting point. Our own research suggests that, in most organizations undertaking HR transformation, some 70 to 80 per cent of the total budget is typically accounted for by the costs of purchasing and delivering HR technology.

Little wonder then that, given such a disproportionate spend on technology, HR transformation projects can take on too much of a technology focus. This can result in a systems-led project where success is defined in terms of testing, data conversion and technical integration rather than delivery of service benefits to customers.

Technology-driven projects may be deemed successful if the technology is delivered on time and to budget; the requisite deliverables are signed off and the handover to 'live running' happens smoothly. Yet a lack of integration with the objectives of the programme may also mean the systems do not provide the critical information needed to support the business partner in the planning process, do not deliver critical functionality in the service centre and do not provide a joined up and integrated end to end process in HR. Clearly the operation may have been a success but the patient is in a bad way!

As discussed in Chapter 2, our own research also suggests that most organizations implementing large scale enterprise resource planning (ERP) solutions in HR (SAP, Oracle, PeopleSoft and so on) successfully deploy less than 25 per cent of the technology's available functionality. This strongly suggests that there is a fundamental disconnect between the perceptions of what will add value in the business and the reality of the service that needs to be delivered.

The reasons for the disconnect lie partly with the software industry who have engaged in a 'functional arms race' in the last few years to build functionality that will give them a competitive advantage and so now have products which in many instances look good in a sales demonstration but which are rarely implemented effectively.

However, the bulk of the 'blame' lies with the organizations themselves for losing sight of the objectives of the programme and failing to link these closely to the design of the technical solution. Our fascination for technology and the sheer scale of expenditure on it can prove a fatal distraction in the implementation process and it is easy to forget that technology is a tool for transformation and not the main driver for it.

In the remainder of this chapter we look at the main methods for articulating the requirements for new technology in a way that relates directly to the strategic objectives of the organization.

Deciding What You Need

'Bold objects require conservative engineering'

James E. Webb

It is both the strength and the weakness of HR systems that they carry a high degree of functionality, are generally available to all and that they are easy to acquire. It is easy, therefore, to create an illusion of progress by going out and buying software without truly understanding how the application will be used by the business.

To make an intelligent start on the assessment of technology needs, a review of current technology failings is likely to reveal a range of issues that constrain the HR function in different ways (see Figure 4.2).

For the shared service centre (SSC), the key considerations will centre on supporting the revised end-to-end process in the operations centre. This will be

Operational Issues	Tactical Issues	Strategic Issues
'It stops us working'	*'It stops us managing'*	*'It stops us changing'*
➢Data are not complete ➢Data are inaccurate ➢We lack basic information ➢We are drowning in paper ➢Data sit in several places ➢System requires a lot of manual intervention ➢People aren't getting paid accurately and on time	➢The system does not cover everyone ➢Only a few people can access data ➢We lack qualitative data in critical areas – for example, skills ➢We have no reporting tools ➢Data on different systems do not agree	➢There is no end-to-end process ➢System drives the process, not the other way around ➢No flexibility to change process ➢System will not support a new organizational model for HR ➢No universal access to PCs – dated IT architecture ➢We cannot forecast trends – we only know what happened in the past

Figure 4.2   Typical issues reducing the impact of technology on the HR function

coupled with a need to drive new types of management information to monitor service performance and financial recharging.

For the HR BP, key considerations at this stage will be how these types of issues impact its clients within the business and how the HR solution will have the potential to help them. The lack of critical qualitative data is likely to be a key issue for senior managers and a key consideration for the BP when defining toolset requirements.

Access to 'key people indicators' relating to pay, benefits and performance is likely to be high on the shopping list for the BP's clients. However, good management information will be irrelevant if HR cannot underpin this with robust core processes relating to pay, resourcing and development, particularly if they are key elements of senior management strategy. Failure to deliver in these areas either now or in the future is always going to be a major barrier to the overall credibility of HR.

WHERE ARE WE HEADED?

Having polled stakeholders at all levels of the organization, a pattern will emerge of the major shortcomings of the current systems. This will provide valuable information to fuel the case for change and to inform the priorities of system delivery.

However, to provide genuine direction, the strategy must also focus on how new systems will support key business objectives. The linkages between business strategy, HR strategy and technology strategy are the most critical foundations for a successful system.

HR operations do not have normally have generic technology requirements. The functional scope requirement of an HR system are influenced by market sector and are further impacted by a range of external factors which alter the demands on people processes and the need for HR data (see Figure 4.3). In short, the business context will heavily influence the system requirements.

The main objective for the HR organization reviewing technology needs is to pin down those factors that have the biggest impact in terms of supporting their client businesses. Ultimately this will ensure that the developed system is rigorously linked to the requirements of the business and that the delivered functionality is prioritized according to the benefit it delivers (rather than on the basis of 'nice to have' features).

The business sector or environment will frequently determine the basic demands of the HR service and supporting technology. Outside factors may change the priorities, scope and functional demands for HR technology.

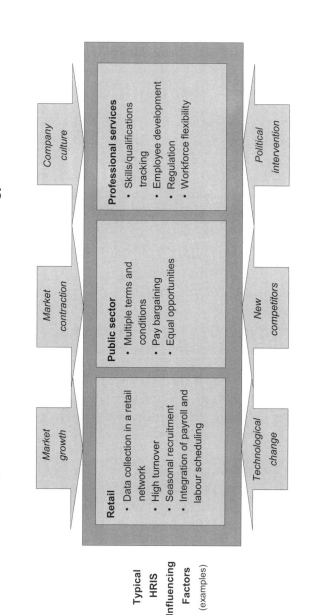

Figure 4.3   Business context

There is no magic formula for making this determination; a good understanding of the organization and its priorities together with good knowledge of the available technology options will be key. The resulting analysis will typically highlight the main components of the HR plan that drive a technology requirement (see Figure 4.4).

Clearly Figure 4.4 is only an example of how the components of business and HR strategy may combine to drive technology requirements, and the HR technology project should start to develop an awareness of this linkage.

The need for access to accurate and timely HR data is in turn dependent on the integrity of the underlying HR process and the effectiveness of the technology that supports it. Any solution that does not address the need for robust core processes or closely integrated people systems is unlikely to produce meaningful management data. Unfortunately this failure may only come to light in the latter stages of the project, so a good understanding of this relationship now is vital.

Management Information

Effective management information (MI) is one of the most important requirements when considering HR information needs. For example, the role of the HR BP demands:

- a clear understanding of the effectiveness and efficiency of operational service;

- the ability to articulate the current status in the business;

- proactivity in the business to support future direction.

The key to providing a high-quality response to the last two items lies in access to high-quality management information and probably reflects one of the principle reasons for investing in the new system. Indeed the lack of basic management information in HR is frequently cited as one of the major frustrations (for example, 'we can't even get a basic headcount'), and systems that do not deliver in this area will rapidly lose credibility with the business. However, despite the importance of MI, it is often not considered in detail as an independent requirement.

Management information is frequently considered as a by-product of good administrative procedures, and this is correct to an extent. An effective recruitment process will compile data about applicants at each stage of the process, building to

The HR strategy takes its cue from the business imperatives of the organization; similarly the HR technology strategy must be able to demonstrate a clear linkage between the HR strategy and the component parts of the proposed system. Set out below is a real example produced for a client organization to demonstrate how key elements of the HR strategy drive technology requirements.

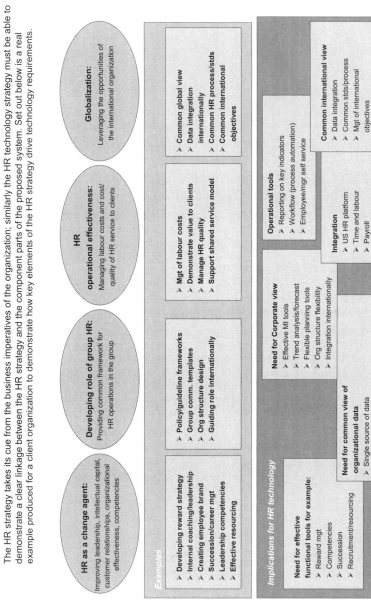

Figure 4.4   HR strategy and implications for HR systems

a complete profile as they become new employees. If the process is managed via a recruitment system, then the system will also be likely to capture management information regarding recruitment cycle times, acceptance/rejection rates and equal opportunities: all potential performance indicators in the recruitment process.

However, whilst this is fine in theory, unless a number of essential system design factors have been considered, then extracting MI in a usable format will not be straightforward and the system may fail to deliver the expected MI benefits. In this section we will explore the different types of MI, who uses them and the key demands on the system; we will also look at the main considerations during design that will impact the successful production of MI.

TYPES OF MI

Requirements for MI have already been considered in Chapter 3, but are repeated here for completeness.

A useful starting point is to consider the types of information that may be defined as 'management information'. Users of MI may range from senior executives to relatively junior staff making operational decisions. Formats may vary from complex standard reports incorporating data from multiple sources to simple queries that may be output to a computer screen. For our purposes we have broken this down into three basic types of MI:

- *Operational MI*: Refers to the day-to-day requirements for information to support ongoing operational processes. This may include queries which clients in the business may expect rapid answers to, or wish to retrieve themselves (for example, 'how many people', 'what is the average turnover', and so on). Failure on the part of the business partner to answer these most basic of queries accurately and promptly will lead to an immediate loss of credibility for both the BP and the system. Key criteria for this type of MI include query tools that are simple to use, rapid access to appropriate systems and data ('I need it now!') and the flexibility to respond to unpredictable questions.

- *Tactical MI*: If operational MI relates to day-to-day operations, tactical MI is about monitoring and analysing HR performance and the effectiveness of HR policies. Examples would include measurement of performance indicators in HR, routine workforce statistics or any area where aggregated data is required to measure some aspect of business performance. Once again, the BP is likely to be required to produce these data or make them accessible to its clients. Whilst this information may not be required instantly it is likely to be needed consistently, in others words to regular schedules, consistent formats and definitions, and formatted to the requirements of the recipients. The flexibility to extract data with different analyses, format outputs and schedule outputs to be produced automatically is likely to be key.

- *Strategic MI*: Many organizations claim the need for strategic data as being their primary driver for investment in new systems. However, interestingly, there appears to be no common view of what constitutes strategic MI in the HR function. If the organization is starting from a baseline of having no MI, then the ability to produce some fairly basic statistics can feel quite strategic. Software suppliers have responded with a range of tools that fall into the 'analytics' category. These are differentiated from standard reporting tools in that they incorporate progress against business objectives into their answers to inform senior management when they are meeting or missing their projected targets. Such analytics tools can be highly effective when coupled with a balanced scorecard approach that consistently monitors a range of performance indicators and spots trends that may lie outside the parameters set by strategic plans. Problem areas or hotspots can be highlighted to executives by means of simple traffic light mechanisms (red for 'off target and requires management action', amber for 'requires close tracking as slippage occurring' and green for 'OK, proceeding to plan') so that executive time can be spent there and not on areas that are working effectively.

Such tools may appear as part of an 'expert analytics' package that provides monitoring and forecasting capability to subject matter experts about their functions. At more senior levels, 'executive analytics' may marry data from a wide range of sources including HR, finance and customer management solutions to focus on business-wide issues.

To produce this type of information requires a significant degree of integration across multiple applications and is increasingly the objective behind integrated, single-supplier approaches to business applications.

All of the software vendors we spoke to cited the growth of interest in 'human capital asset' reporting as a major driver behind their investment in these technologies. A common message was that senior executives are less interested in 'HR data' and are more interested in how it can be combined with other data assets in the organization to answer directional questions for the business.

'Garbage In, Garbage Out?'

1.   *Data standards*: The phrase 'we can't even produce a simple headcount' is regularly repeated in organizations lacking basic HR systems. Whilst this requirement may appear laughably simple, the request is often not as straightforward as it sounds. Accurate headcount is dependent on agreement in a number of areas:

- agreeing what point in time the headcount is taken (headcount may change daily);

- agreeing who is an employee (do you count contractors or staff on maternity leave or sabbatical?);

- agreeing what you are counting (do you count heads or full-time equivalents; how do you count part timers?).

Without agreeing these criteria, any two headcounts will not agree (and yet may both be perfectly accurate). What this illustrates is the need, on a corporate level, to agree reporting and data standards so that critical management information does agree.

Reporting across geographical or organizational lines may require those parts of the organization to agree on basic definitions like 'full time', 'grade', 'total salary' and 'good performance'. These definitions are an essential pre-requisite for production of corporate data but may be constrained where different organizational or geographical units have pursued independent approaches to HR. To achieve required levels of corporate MI it may be necessary to effect a change in definition of common HR data items in different parts of the business.

2.   *Data cleansing*: The poor quality and unreliability of data on existing HR systems is often a primary reason to move. Inevitably implementation requires some consideration of the quality of existing data; how it will be cleaned up and how new data not previously held will be collected and entered to the new system. Inevitably many implementation processes require some form of contact with all current employees to check and collect these data. This can be a time consuming and difficult task but it is important that the BP is rigorous in its demands relating to the quality of data.

3.   *Organization structures*: As previously discussed, organizations may need to consider, for the first time, whether they wish to make investment in maintaining an organization hierarchy to support self-service functionality in HR. However, HR is not the only function that may use self-service and it is not uncommon to find that finance or customer management systems also drive self-service from the organizational structure.

A problem may arise if the organizational structure does not represent the HR view of the organization but is related to, say, a cost code structure. HR will need to ensure that the data on the system can be extracted in a way that is meaningful. For example, there is no point in extracting departmental appraisal data by cost centre if a particular department cannot be isolated in this way.

The purpose of such tools may be summarized as an attempt to standardize the non-standard. Whilst managers may take pride in their organizational capabilities, at the most senior levels there is frequently a requirement to display powers of disorganization; that is, the ability to ask difficult and disruptive questions about the status quo. At this level the functional distinctions of HR, finance and customer data disappear; the BP's job is to ensure that its data are closely aligned and integrated with other forms of data in the organization.

SUMMARY OF CHAPTER MESSAGES

- Successful HR transformation technology delivery is closely dependent on an integrated HR technology strategy. A key requirement for the transformation process is to shift focus from tactical issues such as process mapping or technical analysis and concentrate instead on true criteria for success:

  1. Design a service the business actually needs, engage senior stakeholders early in the process to define design principles for the service.

  2. It is easy for newly formed specialist roles in HR to suffer from each others' failings and hence develop a fragmented 'culture of blame'. Foster an approach to transformation that supports and reinforces the 'one HR' model.

  3. Focus on cost savings alone is unlikely to win the long-term support of the business for the change – expect resistance, manage expectations, be realistic about what will be delivered and focus on the basics.

  4. Develop long-term management disciplines for the new model for HR that embody performance management for the new service, account management to give voice to the customer, performance improvement procedures and financial management processes.

  5. Don't let technology blind you to the underlying requirements or allow the size and scope of technology change to dominate the more fundamental business change.

- Consider failings in the current technology solutions for clues as to the organization's requirements that need to be reflected in the new systems.

- Sector and market influence will be a key determinant of system requirements; there should similarly be a clear linkage between strategic HR imperatives and the defined requirements of the new system.

- Overall system effectiveness will be gauged by the value of the MI it produces; definition of requirements should give careful consideration to management information needs at the operational, tactical and strategic levels.

Project Definition and Start-Up

The Project Approach

Having reviewed the different types of technology that are used within the new model HR function, we will now go on to define the steps involved in implementing HR systems. Achieving the successful delivery of HR transformation technology can be a highly complex undertaking, usually requiring significant changes to business practices. It may take a year or more to complete and involve a large team of people, and should therefore be treated as a project, rather than simply a 'business as usual' task.

A project may be defined as a temporary undertaking to create a unique product or service. It is a discrete and finite piece of work, with fixed start and end points and a clear objective. Projects require dedicated project teams with defined responsibilities, whose actions need to be managed and governed.

As discussed in Part I, many HR technology projects are undertaken in the context of HR transformation and involve the implementation of the full range of HR technologies discussed earlier. A business change initiative of this magnitude would be managed as an entire programme, that is, a collection of related projects.

The key differentiators between programmes, projects and business as usual activity are the degree of change, uncertainty and risk involved. These, in turn, are governed by the scope or breadth of the undertaking, as illustrated in Figure 5.1.

This section of the book will be pitched at the level of the HR transformation technology project rather that of a programme. However, we will highlight cases where additional or different courses of action will be needed if the technology project does form part of a wider programme.

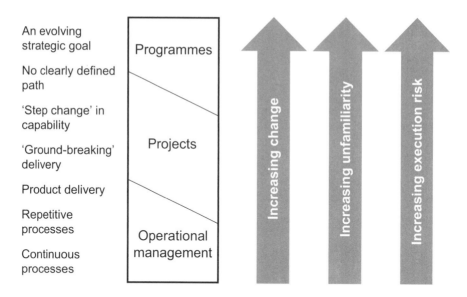

Figure 5.1   Programmes, projects and business as usual

THE MAIN STAGES OF A PROJECT

Whether an HR technology initiative is being managed as a standalone project or as part of a wider programme, the stages involved are similar, as shown in Figure 5.2. This figure also shows the chapter references for each stage, and thus may be used as a route map to refer back to during during your reading.

For consistency we will use the term 'stage' to define the highest level of work breakdown within a project, while the term 'phase' will be used to describe the next level down. For example, the final stage in the project – Technology delivery – comprises three phases: Design/build, Test and Cutover. Note that in different project management methodologies (see Chapter 6) these terms may be reversed or other terms used to describe these concepts.

ESTABLISHING AN HR TRANSFORMATION TECHNOLOGY PROJECT

In order to establish an HR transformation technology project, you need to address the following questions:

- How should the project be governed?
- How should it be sponsored?
- How should it be managed?
- What should the organization of the project team look like?

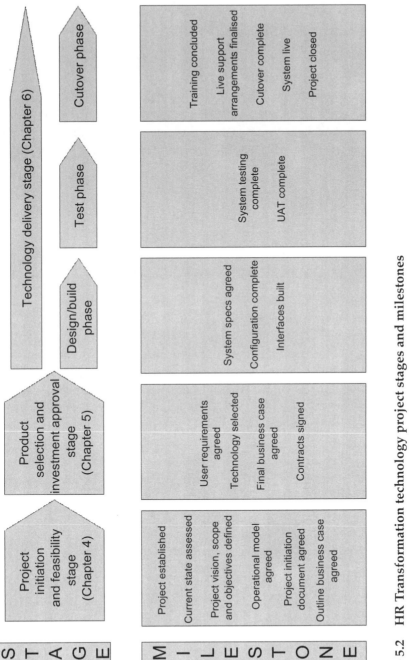

Figure 5.2 HR Transformation technology project stages and milestones

- What, if any, project management methodology should be used?

- How should stakeholders be effectively engaged?

Project Governance and Sponsorship

Governance   Project governance is the means by which senior stakeholders in the client organization oversee the project and make critical decisions such as authorizing commencement of key stages and agreeing major changes. The adoption of new HR technology will have a major impact across and down the organization and will require a group of senior stakeholders to oversee its implementation. These should form a project board or steering committee,[1] membership of which might typically comprise:

- the HR director or senior nominee

- the IT director or senior nominee

- the finance director or senior nominee

- one or more senior executives from the main business areas affected

- the project manager

Project board members should be fully empowered to make the necessary decisions on behalf of their functions or businesses. The project board should meet as regularly as needed, and at a minimum monthly, with special meetings for key sign-off events such as go/no-go decisions. Agendas should be issued in advance and minutes circulated promptly, describing the principal decisions and actions agreed.

Sponsorship   The chair of the project board should also be the project sponsor or champion. The role of the project sponsor is to:

- give high profile support from the top;

- lead the change by example and act as a role model;

- confirm that the organization endorses the change, and will not back out of that decision if the going gets tough;

- grant access to resources for the project, against competing projects;

---

1   From this point on we will use the term 'project board' as favoured by Prince2™, which is the most commonly used project management methodology.

- help the project to overcome operational barriers to success and combat any 'blockers'.

The sponsor should, therefore, be a credible and respected senior executive who can champion the project throughout the organization.

Project Management

Project management is a set of principles, practices and techniques that are applied to the leadership of project teams and to the control of project schedule, costs, quality and risks. Complex projects require excellent management, and the role of project manager is critical to the successful delivery of HR technology. However effective the project's methodology, technology or team, it is unlikely to succeed without a capable project manager.

The project manager's prime objective is to deliver the project within *timescale* and *budget*, and to the required *quality*. Achieving success against these parameters in the case of a large and complex HR transformation technology project involves a wide range of skills, knowledge and experience on the part of the project manager, including:

- authority, credibility and presence;

- the ability to lead, motivate and develop the project team;

- drive and 'stickability';

- a results orientation;

- exceptional communication and influencing skills;

- a high level of judgment and political 'nous';

- the ability to move seamlessly between macro- and micromanagement;

- experience of managing projects of similar type, scale and complexity.

The role of project manager may be sourced internally (perhaps from the HR or IT department) or externally if no one of sufficient calibre is available within the organization. Either way, the project manager is the project's most critical resource, and the right candidate must be chosen. It is not unknown for projects to spend many months on product selection (when the respective advantages of competing packages may be purely marginal), but only a matter of days on attracting an unsuitable project manager, with the inevitable consequence of a costly and painful project failure.

Whilst many HR functions are becoming increasingly capable at managing general projects, project management itself is not a core HR competency. As a result, when considering the selection of key resource such as project manager for the technology project, it may be advisable to appoint from an internal pool or engage external consultancy support.

The Project Team

Roles   With governance arrangements and the project manager in place, the next task is to define the structure and accountabilities of the project team, and start to bring people onto the project. Over the course of a large-scale HR transformation technology implementation, the project team will comprise a number of different types of participants:

- IT staff (or contractors) employed by the client organization to implement software, write interfaces and data conversion programs, carry out technical testing and learn how the system is configured so that they can go on to support it post go-live;

- HR staff seconded by the client organization's HR function to assist with process design, conduct user acceptance testing, resolve data issues and eventually become the 'expert users' of the new system; these may be HR administrators, advisers or specialists and are often referred to as 'SMEs' (subject matter experts);

- external HR technology strategy consultants, to support the client organization through the initiation/feasibility and selection stages.

- (when the software package has been chosen), configurers and technical analysts working for the package supplier, possibly supported by an implementation partner specializing in technical project delivery (the process of package selection is discussed in Chapter 7, together with the merits of using an implementation partner);

- implementation specialists, internal and/or external to the organization, to ensure the thorough accomplishment of complex and detailed tasks such as data capture, data cleanse and cutover planning;

- trainers drawn from the supplier, the implementation partner, or the client organization to conduct the training needs analysis for the new system and prepare and deliver the training content;

- business change, employee relations and communications specialists, sourced from the implementation partner, the client organization or specialist consultancies, to ensure that the business supports is ready for and supports the changes involved.

Project Structure   It is important that all members of a project team have a clear understanding of the project structure, and where they fit into it. To facilitate this, significant projects are usually organized into a number of 'work streams', each reporting into the project manager. A typical structure chart for an HR systems project is shown in Figure 5.3, showing the main accountabilities within each area.

In the case of a wider HR technology programme, some types of roles which are common to a number of projects, for example, business analysts or trainers, may need to be managed as a pooled resource, is made available to individual projects as needed. This is to ensure consistency of approach and effective integration of common deliverables such as the design of end-to-end business processes. It is then a matter for individual project managers to negotiate with programme colleagues to secure sufficient input from these resources. A typical programme structure for a wider initiative, in this case an HR transformation programme, is shown in Figure 5.4.

In this example, the HR transformation programme breaks down into various workstreams, including technology, where the individual systems projects are located. The structure for each HR technology project will be broadly similar to the standalone example shown earlier, including reporting to a dedicated project board in the case of the larger projects such as CRM and HR/payroll.

Resourcing the Team   Whilst a full project team is not required on day one, it is necessary to acquire sufficient resources to carry out the project initiation and feasibility stage, which requires the production of an extensive set of 'paper' deliverables to ensure that the project has a sound platform. For this stage, the project manager will require the support of workstream leaders plus specialists sourced from the IT and HR functions.

HR management will need to consider seconding one or more HR people onto the project on a full-time basis, balancing the needs of the project with those of the current HR operation. Full-time secondments of key users to

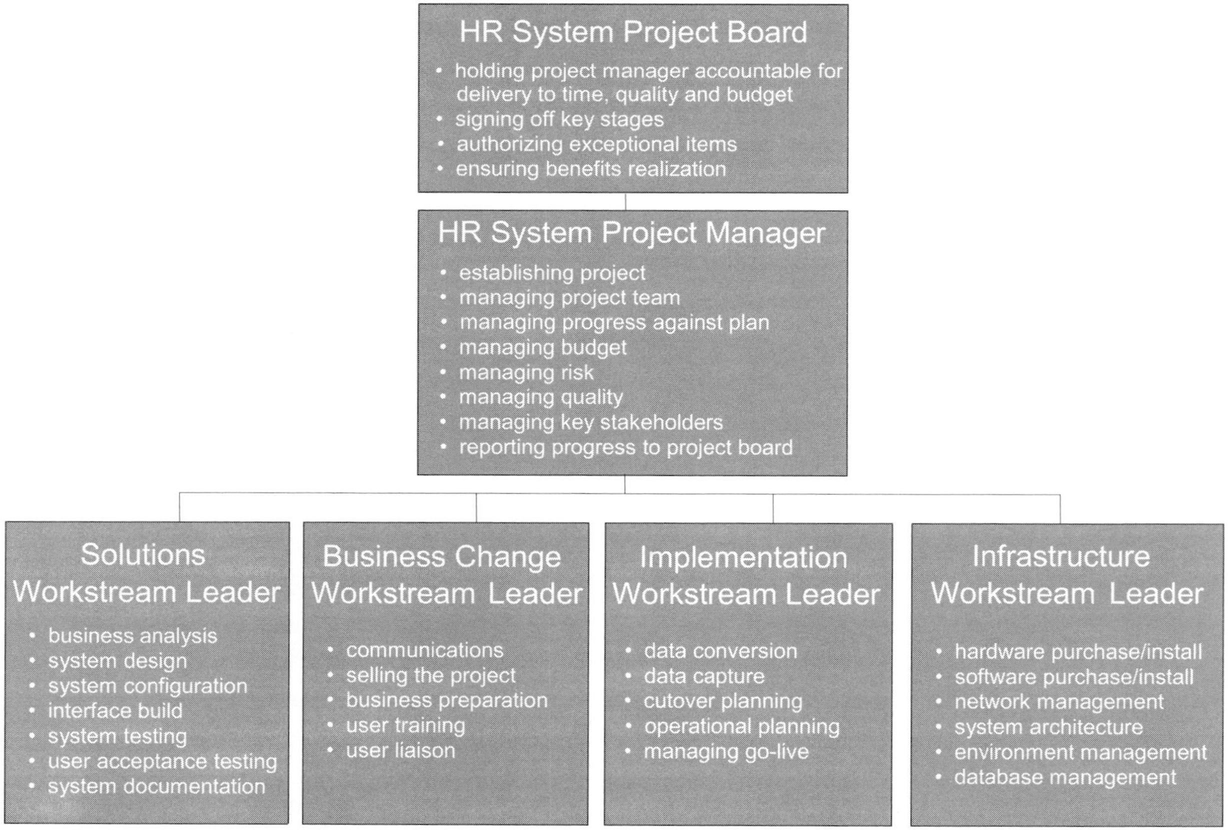

HR System Project Board
- holding project manager accountable for delivery to time, quality and budget
- signing off key stages
- authorizing exceptional items
- ensuring benefits realization

HR System Project Manager
- establishing project
- managing project team
- managing progress against plan
- managing budget
- managing risk
- managing quality
- managing key stakeholders
- reporting progress to project board

Solutions Workstream Leader
- business analysis
- system design
- system configuration
- interface build
- system testing
- user acceptance testing
- system documentation

Business Change Workstream Leader
- communications
- selling the project
- business preparation
- user training
- user liaison

Implementation Workstream Leader
- data conversion
- data capture
- cutover planning
- operational planning
- managing go-live

Infrastructure Workstream Leader
- hardware purchase/install
- software purchase/install
- network management
- system architecture
- environment management
- database management

Figure 5.3 HR system project structure

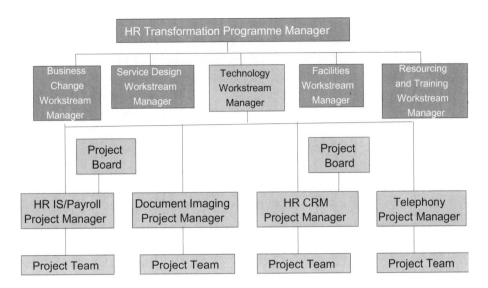

Figure 5.4   HR transformation programme structure

large projects are the most effective approach, otherwise the demands of the individuals' 'day jobs' tend to prevent them from providing the level of input needed. The involvement of the sponsor is often instrumental in 'unblocking' the release of SMEs from the business when they are leaving a 'day job' to be backfilled, with the associated 'operational hassle'.

It is also sensible at this stage to consider using external consultants specializing in HR transformation and systems strategy who can add expertise in areas such as HR organization, service design and technology deployment and integration. This will ensure that key stage deliverables, such as the vision, business model, project initiation document and business case, are validated against best practice.

At this stage, the project will need to secure accommodation for the team. It will also be necessary to implement a project office to ensure that formal documents are lodged in a project library with proper version control, and that basic office services and project support are available to the project team.

Project Management Methodologies

A large-scale HR transformation technology project may provide some participants with their first experience of using a structured project management methodology. During recent years the science of systems implementation has progressed significantly. Projects no longer need to be designed from scratch but rely instead on standard and proven methodologies (the 'cookbooks' of system delivery).

It is likely that any implementation partner will have their own project management methodology, as indeed may the client organization's own IT function. Many public sector organizations, and increasingly many private sector companies, are adopting Prince2 as their project management methodology of choice. Prince was developed originally for large public sector IT projects, but has now been made generic so that it can be applied to IT or non-IT projects of varying scale in any type of organization.

Essentially, Prince2 and other methodologies of its type deliver a set of processes, tools and facilities which together form a framework for sound project management discipline. As such they:

- stipulate effective governance arrangements so that key stakeholders are active in overseeing the project, but in a time-effective manner;

- require clear project structures and roles so that everyone knows what they and others are doing;

- require effective project definition and a robust business case;

- provide for realistic project planning and rigorous monitoring of tasks, and of quality;

- provide techniques for disciplined project control such as risk, issue and change management and management reporting;

- insist upon formal sign-off to one project stage before the next stage can be initiated;

- require regular referral back to the business case and original project definition to ensure that the benefits are not being compromised as the project proceeds.

Generally, project management methodologies help good project managers to perform better, but they need to be applied knowingly and rarely help bad project managers to perform satisfactorily. If use of such a methodology is a requirement of the HR technology project, all members of the project team should be briefed in its application. It should soon become apparent that the methodology is grounded in common sense and sound management practice, albeit cloaked in a little jargon. This is also an opportunity, of course, for HR professionals, particularly in the change management areas, to acquire valuable new skills in common use across the business, consistent with the function's drive towards commercialization.

Stakeholder Management

At an early stage it is important for the project sponsor and project manager to identify the major stakeholder and how best to secure and retain their commitment throughout the project. Clearly, the members of the project board will be key players, but a wide range of other people may have varying degrees of 'skin' in the success of the project for, example:

- senior executives whose businesses are not represented on the project board;

- internal audit, for example where a new payroll system is being implemented;

- specialist IT areas, such as IT architecture and security, particularly where the project involves the implementation of software that is new to the organization;

- trade unions, who will be keen to understand any impact which the project might have on staffing levels.

In each case it is important to assess the degree of influence that each party can have on the project and then to ascertain the minimum amount of effort needed to secure and maintain their buy-in. A useful tool for carrying out such an assessment is shown in Figure 5.5.

Having identified how much attention each stakeholder requires, it is then necessary to determine the most effective way of managing contact with them, for example, a weekly meeting or phone call, ensuring that they receive project board agendas and minutes and so on. It is also important to identify 'blockers and movers' (those that hinder or help) in order to develop strategies for managing these very different types of relationships as well identifying those within the programme best suited to handling them.

With the project up and running, the team can address the remaining tasks of the initiation and feasibility stage.

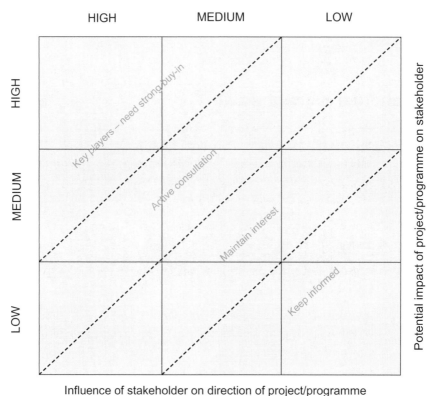

Figure 5.5   Stakeholder influence matrix

Conducting a Current State Assessment

Before attempting to define the solution, it is necessary to confirm what the problem is. This involves carrying out a current state assessment, as a basis for achieving a consensus among the major stakeholders as to what the project needs to fix.

ASSESSING THE CONTEXT – WHY DOES ANYTHING NEED TO CHANGE?

As discussed in Part I, there are a range of circumstances in which new or replacement HR technology may be required, depending upon how the HR function is organized, its current deployment of technology, where it is aiming to be and how ready it is for change. Most organizations embarking upon an HR technology project will be faced with one of two broad scenarios: greenfield or brownfield, probably depending upon whether an HR shared service centre (SSC) is being created.

Creating an HR Shared Service Centre (Greenfield Scenario)

Many organizations are considering, or are already in the process of implementing, an HR SSC:

- as a standalone initiative, involving the consolidation and re-design of HR administration and advice;

- as part of a wholesale HR transformation initiative, affecting the entire HR function;

- as part of an organization-wide initiative, aimed at establishing joint shared service operations for a range of back-office functions (for example, HR, finance and procurement).

In such 'greenfield' scenarios, a major HR technology programme is likely to be required, the scope of which might include new CRM, telephony and document imaging systems plus perhaps a replacement HR IS/payroll solution.

Implementing Replacement HR Technology (Brownfield Scenario)

There will also be cases where the scope of change is more limited, for example, to replace a failing or outdated system (for example, payroll) without any consequent major organizational change. In such a 'brownfield' scenario, it may be sufficient to treat the technology replacement initiative as a single project, although a programme approach may still be needed if more than one major system involved.

INTERNAL ASSESSMENT – WHERE DOES IT HURT?

One approach to conducting a current state assessment is to focus on how the organization is being damaged by failings in HR technology. As previously discussed in Chapter 4, useful model for carrying out this assessment is shown in Figure 5.6.

Existing data may already be available to inform the assessment, for example, performance against service level agreements, feedback from businesses, staff surveys and so on. This can be augmented by holding workshops or focus groups of key users (HR staff, line managers and employees) to highlight and examine the major deficiencies.

EXTERNAL ASSESSMENT – BENCHMARKING

Having identified that a problem may exist, it is useful to benchmark the performance of the client organization's HR function, processes and technology,

Operational Issues *'It stops us working'*	Tactical Issues *'It stops us managing'*	Strategic Issues *'It stops us changing'*
▪ data incomplete ▪ data inaccurate ▪ lack of basic info ▪ 'drowning in paper' ▪ data fragmented ▪ manual intervention ▪ people aren't getting paid accurately and on time	▪ system does not cover everyone ▪ only a few people can access data ▪ lack of qualitative data in critical areas – for example, skills ▪ no generic access to reporting tools ▪ data on different systems do not agree	▪ no end-to-end process ▪ system drives the process not the other way around ▪ no flexibility to change process ▪ system will not support new organizational models ▪ no universal access to PCs – dated IT architecture ▪ cannot forecast trends – 'we only know what happened in the past'

Figure 5.6　Impact of poor systems

against industry standards. Benchmarking data may be obtained from consultancies, providing comparative metrics analysed by size, sector and so on. As with all benchmarking, the danger is in comparing apples with oranges, and it is most important to ensure that all qualifications attached to the data provided are fully understood.

It may be advisable at this stage to use management consultants in a more general capacity, to give an external perspective on HR operational performance against best practice in terms of organization, service design and technology. They should also be able to provide a list and provisional assessment of the main technology packages, their suppliers and potential implementation partners.

The current state assessment should have highlighted where the major problems reside, from both internal and external perspectives. This sense of what is lacking can now be fed into the task of defining the required solution.

Defining Project Vision, Scope and Objectives

Before getting too far into detailed deliverables such as the project initiation documents (PID) and the business case, it is important to hammer a few stakes in the ground to get basic agreement on what the project is about, in terms of its vision, scope and objectives.

VISION

A project vision statement should be a succinct yet meaningful expression of what the project is there to achieve. An effective vision statement serves a number of purposes:

- it defines 'the reason why we are doing this';

- it is the 'heart and soul' of the project;

- it is the main reason why the team want to carry on when things get tough;

- it is the main driver behind everything that follows, as illustrated in Figure 5.7.

An example of a simple vision statement for an employee self-service project might be as follows:

'To introduce an automated self-service facility for administrative processes such as recording absence and overtime, which will eliminate duplication and be easier to use than the current arrangement.'

This example satisfies the criteria for an effective vision statement shown above. It is succinct in that the vision is described in one sentence. It is meaningful because it defines what is to be done, that is, automation, and the type of operations to be covered – administrative processes such as absence and overtime recording. It also offers clear and measurable goals:

- elimination of duplication, which can be measured objectively;

Figure 5.7   Project Vision

- making it easier to use than the current arrangement, which can be measured subjectively by getting user feedback or objectively by analysing the old and new systems in order to compare the amount of data entry, error rates or the time taken to complete each process.

In summary, a well-crafted vision is an excellent tool for motivating the team and controlling the direction of the project.

SCOPE

At the same time as describing the vision, it is important to define the scope of the new solution. An effective scoping statement for an HR system needs to cover a range of variables:

- *functional scope*: applications covered, for example, recruitment, may be further defined by listing the main processes concerned;

- *business scope*: which employees across the whole organization will be in scope;

- *user scope*: what type of users will be included, for example, HR BPs, HR SSC, HR strategy, line managers, employees, pensioners, applicants and so on, and broad numbers in each case;

- *system scope*: which systems it proposes to replace;

- *integration scope*: what types of new or replacement interfaces are likely to be needed;

- *data scope*: for example, what historical data are likely to require conversion, what new data may need to be captured.

It is equally important to state what is out of scope in order to avoid any misunderstanding. For example, in the case of an HR CRM system, all employees and applicants may be in scope but pensioners may be out of scope, at least for the first release of the new system. The scope may evolve as the project proceeds, but this should be managed via change control, rather than merely being allowed to happen. The use of change control in order to avoid 'scope drift' is discussed under project controls in Chapter 8.

OBJECTIVES

To complete the outline picture, it is necessary to define the objectives of the project, for example:

1. to deliver a solution which satisfies the scope and vision defined above;

2. to achieve delivery within the required timeframe and quality criteria, as set out in the project initiation document;

3. to achieve delivery within budget, as set out in the business case;

4. to realize the project's benefits as set out in the business case;

5. to minimize risk and disruption to the existing system and operation.

At this stage, objectives 2 to 4 cannot be defined more precisely because the PID and business case have yet to be finalized.

Getting Sign-off from the Project Board

However, at this early stage, these objectives, together with the project vision and scope, provide an essential framework for the project. It is therefore advisable to clear this, together with the current state assessment, with the project board before proceeding too far with work on the remaining initiation and feasibility stage deliverables, which are discussed in Chapter 6.

SUMMARY OF CHAPTER MESSAGES

- The delivery of HR transformation technology is a large-scale undertaking requiring the establishment of a project, which is a discrete and finite piece of work involving a dedicated project team.

- Projects require strong governance to ensure that delivery is overseen by senior stakeholders in the form of a project board or steering committee, which should be responsible for taking all major decisions, including signing off key project stages.

- The project manager is the most important member of the project team, and every effort should be made to ensure that the project manager has the required level of skills, knowledge and experience.

- It is not essential to use a formal project management methodology. However, it is vital to adopt the underlying disciplines inherent in all good methodologies: strong governance, clear structures, roles and responsibilities, realistic and rigorous planning and effective management controls.

- A current state assessment should be carried out, benchmarked against external best practice, to demonstrate to key stakeholders why the project is needed. From this an outline vision scope and objectives should be developed.

Project Initiation and   CHAPTER
Feasibility

6

Defining the Proposed Operational Model

Having conducted the current state assessment and defined the project's vision, scope and objectives, some project methodologies would go from here direct to the production of the Project Initiation Document (PID) and business case. The experience of the authors suggests that to do this is to risk alienating key stakeholders by failing to answer fundamental questions like:

- What is the solution going to look like?

- How is it going to work, from a business standpoint?

- How will it work technically?

- How do I know it will be capable of delivering the stated benefits?

This is where the operational model comes in. Although these types of questions will not be fully addressed until after the software has been configured and the design finalized, it is important during the initiation and feasibility stage to paint a robust and credible picture of how the new world will look, including the likely impact of the new technology. This will add ballast to the project framework defined by the vision, scope and objectives, and demonstrate that the main business and technical implications of the new model have been thought through to a reasonable level of detail.

This is particularly important in a greenfield scenario (see Chapter 5) where the future model is likely to be considerably different from the current operation. But even in the case of a more modest brownfield project such as a system replacement, a well fleshed-out future model is still needed to give confidence to stakeholders that the new, more automated solution will work both technically and from a business perspective.

CONTENT OF THE 'OPERATIONAL MODEL DESIGN DOCUMENTS'

Before going on to describe the in-scope business processes, it is important to set the scene. Hence the introduction might restate the vision, scope and objectives, and go on to propose some key business design principles that might inform the intended operating model, for example:

Standardization

Multiple versions of the same process add complexity to the operational design. They also require additional configuration effort. From both a business model and a project perspective, it is better to have one standard version of each process. By flagging this early, it may be possible to eliminate duplicating factors such as process variations before detailed design commences. It may even be possible to address issues such as multiple competency models or varying terms and conditions, although the lead-time for this will be greater, particularly if negotiations with trade unions are involved. At the same time it is very important to position 'standardization' correctly with the business so that it is not simply seen as a 'one size fits all approach' and that modifications can be made to suit specific and unique business needs. Modifications of this type are permissible within the standard configuration parameters in most products, although all such requests should be carefully reviewed and challenged to fully understand the costs and the implications on other parts of the project.

Data entered once only, at source

In principle, it is most efficient and effective for data to be entered into a system by the data originator. By this means, both duplication of effort and the risk of transposition errors are avoided. Taking HR administration as an example, this principle works well in the case of regular transactions (for example, managers entering overtime) or simple ones (such as, staff entering change of address details). It is less effective in more complex or irregular processes such as entering maternity leave details, which may be best achieved by the relevant forms being completed manually by staff or managers and sent to the SSC for data entry.

E-Enablement

The above principle must be supported by ease of system access and usage. For self-service to be effective, the process must be facilitated by excellent e-enablement whereby the system is widely available via a web browser and the screens (or 'e-forms') are easy to understand, access and use.

Outline Business Process Model

The proposed business process model should include a brief summary of the in-scope processes including who will carry out some of the key tasks in the process and how the new technology is intended to support the new operation. At this early stage, this can be presented as a table or even a set of flowcharts. Either way, this will flesh out the vision created earlier by describing, albeit still at a high level:

- how the new operation is expected to work;

- who will be involved;

- what they will be required to do;

- how the technology will help them.

It will also start to quantify the level of business change that the project will bring to customers such as HR staff, employees and line managers.

As an example, let us assume that a programme is under way which will (a) deliver a new HR shared service centre (SSC) and (b) implement a replacement HR system which will introduce organization management to the company. Table 6.1 is a high-level description of the process for updating the HR system with details of a departmental reorganization.

Table 6.1   Process for updating the HR system with details of a departmental reorganization

Line Manager	HR SSC (OM Team)
Documents required changes to structure (e.g. by annotating print-out of previous structure chart)	
Sends details (e.g. annotated chart) to HR SSC, and/or phones them	
	Updates HR system organisation structure and informs line manager that changes have been entered
Views updated structure chart on-line, and contacts HR SSC if further corrections are required	

This simple table may serve to head off a number of concerns among stakeholders, for example:

- Will line managers need to know how to update organizational details on the system? (No)

- Will they need to complete complex forms? (No – they can send in amended sheets or talk the changes through over the phone)

- Will they need to use the system? (Yes, but only to view it)

- Will the system show them organizational data on line? (Yes, in the form of an organizational chart)

- Who will maintain the data? (The HR SSC)

- Will they be equal to this specialized task? (Yes – this work will be done by a dedicated team)

In this example, the line manager and the HR function are both entering a new and different world, and the table should give the type of assurances that stakeholders will want before being prepared to sign off the business case, even if it looks financially sound.

This forms the start of the 'process documentation pack', which will be developed and deepened progressively as software is selected and the detailed design completed, for example with process flowcharts backed by descriptions of each task. Eventually the pack will contain detailed procedures and work instructions, standard letters, e-forms, e-mails and so on. Even at this early stage, it may be useful to describe one or two key processes to a more detailed level to illustrate more fully how the proposed solution will work and to demonstrate robustness of thought.

The impact on any processes which may appear to be out of scope also needs to be addressed, given the highly integrated nature of HR processes and also their relationship to processes which may lie outside the HR function, for example, payroll accounting.

Outline Technical Model

It is important to demonstrate how the proposed solution will look and work from a technical as well as business standpoint, and the following points should be included in a high level technical model:

PACKAGE VERSUS IN-HOUSE SOLUTION

In the HR technology arena at least, it is rare these days to have to build IT solutions from scratch, so a package solution would normally be assumed. An important system design principle should be that the solution will be achieved by configuring rather than customizing the package. This means using the features provided by the package rather than modifying the underlying software to achieve something different. The disadvantages with customizations are that they (a) take longer to build than configuration (b) will not be supported by the supplier and (c) may cease to work when the supplier releases periodic upgrades to its software. Therefore project managers should think very carefully before recommending to their project boards that any HR package should be customized. It may be simpler to change the organization's business processes – after all, the better packages are based on best practice foundations.

IT ARCHITECTURE

An outline statement of IT architecture requirements is needed, covering:

- *Opportunities*: For example, where a software supplier offers an HR or CRM system which may satisfy all of HR's requirements at a discounted rate;

- *Constraints*: For example, that the solution must use a particular database product;

- *Security and access issues*: For example, must the solution conform to the requirement that users should only enter their ID and password once to gain appropriate access to all the IT systems they use? (known as the 'single sign-on' principle);

- *How the new system will relate to adjacent systems and the interface requirements*: Including details of numbers and types of such systems (for example, batch, web services and so on);

- *How management information needs might be met*: For example, via standard reports, custom reports, augmenting the organization's data warehouse with the data from the new HR systems;

- *How the solution fits in to the organization's overall IT strategy.*

INFRASTRUCTURE

This section should describe:

- an initial estimate of the type and number of servers that are expected to be required by the new system, bearing in mind that it will require various 'environments', for example, development, testing, training and live (or 'production');

- the number of PCs needed, and whether web browser or full system access is required, depending on the type of user;

- the communications infrastructure describing the role of local and wide area networks, including the organization's Internet access (TCP/IP) network, any bandwidth implications, the need for external secure lines (for example, for applicants or staff accessing the system from home or on the road using laptops and so on).

LIVE SUPPORT

When operational the system will need to be supported by various parties:

- local IT support, for PCs and LANs (unless handled centrally by a help desk);

- central IT support for servers, WANs/TCP/IP networks, environments, database, interfaces and so on; the IT department may also provide first line help desk support for queries relating to the new system's functionality (unless there is a front line local application support facility, for example, provided by the HR SSC, in which case central IT will provide second line support);

- The package supplier for second (or third) line application support.

As with the business process model, the outline technical model may change during product selection and design. However, at this early stage, it should offer sufficient confidence that significant thought has been applied to how the project's vision might be realized technically.

SUMMARY

The operational model should paint a vivid picture of how the solution will solve the problems highlighted by the current state assessment. It should be of sufficient depth to answer the fundamental questions that may be posed at this stage by stakeholders representing the business and IT. As such, it should support the process of gaining approval to the project initiation document (PID) and the outline business case. Let us finally examine these last two documents, starting with the PID.

Preparing the Project Initiation Document (PID)

The purpose of the project initiation document (PID) is to describe what the project aims to achieve, why it is necessary, how it will be delivered, who will do it, when each stage will be done by, and how it will be controlled. Its content, much of which will have already been prepared, is described below.

CONTEXT

This provides some background to the project: why it is needed, what it will cover (and not cover), what it will look like, and what are the main assumptions, risks and constraints. It may consist of the following headings:

- *Background*: Summary of existing position, problems highlighted by the current state assessment, progress of project to date;

- *Vision, scope and objectives*: Describes what the project is trying to achieve; the operational model could be appended to provide greater depth to this;

- *Assumptions*: For example, that a package, rather than an in-house built solution, will be implemented;

- *Risks*: Key risks currently anticipated and how it is planned to mitigate them. For example, there might be a risk that insufficient HR staff will be available to be seconded onto the project, to be mitigated by hiring temporary staff to cover their routine jobs;

- *Constraints*: For example, some organizations take the view that a new payroll system should not go live between January and April because of the competing demands of implementing the annual pay awards and tax year-end demands.

PROJECT APPROACH

This section describes the approach that the project intends to apply to the remaining stages:

- *Selection*: For example, outlining how a preferred software supplier will be selected or stating whether/why it is planned to use an implementation partner (see Chapter 7). This secton could also cover how the project will work with one or more suppliers to help finalize the business case.

- *Design/build*: How will design be conducted (for example, use of requirements workshops and checkpoint meetings for users to review the configuration), who will develop the interfaces and so on. This might be a good point to restate key design principles, such as standardization and no product customization.

- *Testing*: For example, what will be the planned approach to user testing, how many parallel runs will be undertaken and will this be based on a sample of records or the whole population?

- *Training*: Containing outline training needs analysis and proposed approach, tools, location, resources and so on.

- *Business change and communications*: Including a high-level assessment of the impact that the new operational model will have on those affected and what steps can be taken to ensure that the business is ready for the change.

- *Implementation phasing*: For example, will all applications be launched across the entire organization or will roll-out be phased in? Will there be a pilot? Will there be implementation waves or will the whole organization go live simultaneously?

- *Data conversion*: What approach will be taken to converting the historical data that has been identified as needing to be transferred from the old to the new system?

- *Data capture requirements*: Will any new data be needed (for example, position details if organizational management is being implemented for the first time)? Will any existing data need to be cleansed (for example, e-mail addresses in an HR CRM project); and how will this be achieved?

- *Proposed technical approach*: How will the different technical environments and resources be made available and deployed during the project; will some of the coding be outsourced?

- *Major cutover issues*: Will any significant interim arrangements be needed immediately before, during or after launch?

PROJECT PLAN

Many projects fail because project timescales prove to be far too optimistic. Starting with the major deliverables, stages and milestones, this section describes the project plan together with the factors that govern it.

- *Major deliverables*: The key outputs from each stage, for example, user requirements document, system specification, system configuration and so on.

- *Key stages and milestones*: A high-level plan showing the main stages (see example project plan in Appendix A) with their start and end dates, and the major milestones which each stage will accomplish (for example, package chosen and purchased).

- *Tasks and resources*: A more detailed breakdown of each stage showing the main tasks and who will do them, with resource estimates. At the very least a detailed plan for the next stage should be available by this point (if lengthy, the full project plan could be appended to the PID).

- *Dependencies*: the key dependencies both within the project (for example, user acceptance testing cannot start until the system test has been signed off) and external to the project (for example, installing the servers depends upon the new data centre being built).

- *Critical path*: Highlighting the longest dependent series of tasks which cannot slip without delaying go-live. For example, if designing, specifying and developing the interfaces constitutes the longest set of linked tasks in the design/build stage and they occupy the entire duration of that stage, then they will form part of the critical path.

- *Contingencies*: Based on the above, describe how the project plan could be flexed to cope with critical difficulties. For example, it might be possible to descope certain processes or interfaces without major detriment to the business case.

- *Quality:* Showing the measures proposed to ensure that quality assurance is planned into each key stage and deliverable, and how will this be monitored (a full quality plan could be appended to the PID).

PROJECT GOVERNANCE AND CONTROL

The topics of project organization and governance and the use of methodologies were covered in Chapter 5; however, other factors for consideration here include the following:

- *Controls*: Various control mechanisms are available to project managers and should be used appropriately, even if a formal methodology is not being followed. These include risk, issue and change management, progress reporting mechanisms, and regular reviews of progress against plan and budget. These will be explored more fully under system delivery (Chapter 8), but it is important that the PID describes whether and how they will be used.

- *Administration*: Describes how the project office will operate and how the project document library will be maintained (important given the likely weight of design and other project documentation).

We now have a clear statement of the problem, the proposed solution, and how the project intends to deliver it. The final task in the project initiation and feasibility stage is to prepare an initial cut of the business case.

Preparing The Business Case[1]

The business case is one area where there may be large variations between organizations in terms of approach, the level of detail included and the rigour with which the cost-benefit case is made. For organizations that view the HR function as an overhead, then the arguments for technology tend to be focused around reducing that overhead: 'How can we reduce HR headcount or other operating costs?'. However, in organizations that value the strategic contribution of HR and seek to drive increased performance and competitive behaviour through the use of best practice people policies, the case for technology may be centred on the enablement of an HR transformation process.

Generally, the business case will be used to drive a decision at senior levels on whether the proposed expenditure on HR transformation technology can be justified and whether the project can proceed. The main headings we will therefore consider in relation to the construction of the business case are as follows:

- use of third parties to support the business case

---

1   Hunter, I., Saunders, J., Boroughs, A. and Constance, S. (2006), *HR Business Partners* (Aldershot, Gower).

- preparing the cost model

- the benefits case

- selling the case to the board

THE USE OF THIRD PARTIES TO SUPPORT THE BUSINESS CASE

The initiation of the business case is frequently the first point at which the organization will engage with outside parties in relation to the project.

The need to identify sound cost estimates will involve obtaining quotes on software licenses, technology architecture and implementation services from suppliers. Consideration of long-term support for the application may require an examination of the external application and architecture market. Similarly, if the new service delivery model for HR is dependent upon an outsourced business process model then these suppliers and their technology offerings may also be factored into the equation.

Most suppliers of technology services will engage account teams at senior levels in the organization and make a substantial year-round investment in understanding the business context of new projects and are well positioned to support this type of initiative.

However, it is important to realize that, as the requirement for HR information and process support is explored in more detail, so the complexity of the solution may also grow. For example, opening up self-service applications to remote locations to facilitate organizational change in HR may demand consideration of the business's requirements for new software, hardware and network infrastructure as well as hosting and support. It is highly unlikely that a project team working solely with internal resources will be able to scope and cost a solution accurately for the business case. Engagement with the relevant vendor account teams to understand their offerings, costs and dependencies will be crucial.

Third-party suppliers can also provide an invaluable source of information to support the planning and business case process. As well as giving information on costs and available discounts they will frequently be able to provide examples of how other organizations have tackled similar issues and the type of benefit they were able to realize.

To deliver complex system integration projects, many consultancies maintain teams of consultants dedicated to a particular solution and their own sales teams will often work in close alliance with those of the software supplier. A a business may have no idea that a particular consultancy is working so closely with the software supplier who recommended them or vice versa. Therefore, the engagement of a truly 'independent adviser' should be carefully examined.

An independent adviser should not receive payment from a supplier; should not be reliant upon that supplier for a major part of their business and should be able to provide clear guidance and opinions on the way forward. A consultant who will not come off the fence is of little use to the project team, who will need clear answers as to the relative strengths and weaknesses of the solutions offered.

PREPARING THE COST MODEL

Pinning down the component parts of the costs of a solution can be complex and frustrating work.

On the one hand, suppliers, whilst keen to push the advantages of their product, may be reluctant to present costs for a wide range of modules for fear of sinking the business case. On the other hand, an internal team may take the view that the costs should be presented as conservatively as possible, as building up the costs on the basis of the 'worst case scenario' may make the project unviable before it gets off the ground.

Clearly, a middle way is required that provides a thorough and honest appraisal of the solution costs whilst ensuring that the principal variables affecting costs have been pinned down as far as possible.

Cost components that should be included are as follows:

- *Software licence:* Providers typically sell licences to organizations wishing to use the different modules of their software. Additional costs may be incurred for the use of the supplier's underlying database products and management information tools. 'Bundled' deals should be looked at closely to ensure proper fit with the timing of the project. For example, it may be 12 or 18 months before the licences for some modules need to be 'drawn down' – an issue that can make a difference to the business case. Costs associated with the use of third-party licences will also need to be looked at.

- *Technical architecture*: The design and configuration of large-scale networks and support infrastructure are specialized skills in their own right and care should be taken that the project engages the appropriate technical resources in order to avoid the underestimation of costs going into the business case.

- *Application development and delivery*: This covers a wide range of activities associated with the delivery of the new solution. This relates predominantly to people costs and is particularly important if third-party rather than internal resources are to be used. Typically, implementation of a full scope ERP solution will require support in the following areas:

  - application design (establishing how the application will need to be configured to meet the demands of the business)

  - development (configuring and customising the core application to meet the design criteria)

  - testing

  - data conversion

  - training

  - deployment of the system in separate geographical locations

The Benefits Case

In some organizations the benefit case for investment in HR technology is taken as read with it simply being a case of defining how the functions and information provided by the new system will work in support of the accepted HR strategy. In others it is an uphill struggle mainly related to the historical perception of HR as a predominantly administrative function providing little added value.

However, making the case for investment is not as difficult as might first appear if it is tied effectively to other planned changes in the HR organization; moving from a traditional to shared service model is of course the most striking example.

HR system benefits usually fall into the following three categories:

- *Hard benefit*: Hard benefit is defined as strictly tangible cash savings arising directly from the introduction of new technology. 'Tangible' may be defined as costs that reside in a clearly identifiable cost centre that can be reduced by a specified amount in coming years.

- *Headcount savings:* Headcount savings can be realised when staff numbers are reduced as a direct result of implementing the new system. Typically, this is from savings arising from isolated improvements in operational efficiency or on a larger scale through a reorganization of the way in which HR services are delivered. More significant savings are achievable through, for example, the reorganization into a SSC offering the opportunity to re-engineer 'end to end' processes with the potential to realise savings from 'hidden HR activity' undertaken by line managers and staff. It is not unusual for savings of 25 to 30 per cent to be achieved if transformation is successfully delivered.

- *Technology savings*: The decommissioning of existing systems in HR is likely to generate some level of cost saving in its own right. An important consideration in the replacement of legacy systems is the current cost of ownership, where the cost of support and maintenance can be very high. In particular, costs associated with current systems in the following related areas:

  - software licence maintenance and support

  - internal and contracted IT support costs

  - hardware/server maintenance.

Other areas of less obvious benefit opportunity are as follows:

- *Cost avoidance*: If it can be argued that 'Y' can be saved if 'X' is spent and this can be identified as a budgeted cost then this can be included in the business case. A typical example would be the avoidance of a planned upgrade to an existing platform.

- *Reduction in third-party costs*: The use of third-party suppliers to support critical or high volume activities is a regular feature of many HR functions. Investing in new technology may afford opportunities to reconsider these contracts, for example, recruitment/training/payroll and pensions, and the costs associated with them. A good example would be that the use of better quality/more sensitive operational HR information to track the effectiveness of suppliers will bring cost reduction and service improvement opportunities.

- *Opportunity benefit*: Many of the benefits offered by a modern HR information system will relate to new opportunities to realize improvements in process or service. For example, automation of the production of candidate correspondence and use of third-party resources to support the candidate sifting process of a tourism and leisure company resulted in 40 per cent savings in the first year. However, not all of these improvements will result in direct cost savings of this type; some will create the opportunity to make new savings as a result of some additional action, with the classic examples of reducing staff turnover and absence management being of greatest potential.

- *Service level improvements*: A central part of any business case will be tying the technology investment to the positive impact on the quality of HR service delivery, particularly in the following areas:

  - improved data integrity and accuracy;

  - faster response to queries – more accurate, better informed decisions;

  - faster response to requests for MI;

  - more effective trend analysis and the potential to initiate proactive management;

  - improved service levels to external candidates;

  - better focused and targeted training initiatives;

  - reducing risk by eliminating service failures and missed data entry through error;

  - alignment of HR to the business agenda, providing the opportunity to create dedicated resource for generalist advice/ centralization of operational tasks.

'SELLING TO THE BOARD' – GETTING SIGN-OFF TO THE PROJECT INITIATION AND FEASIBILITY STAGE

Getting sign-off to the project initiation and feasibility stage is the responsibility of the project manager, and will include the production of the operational model, the PID and the business case, and presenting them to the project board for approval.

In many cases the business case will, ultimately, be signed off at board or executive committee level given the level of investment involved. The project manager is accountable for ensuring that the cost and benefit data are consolidated into a formal financial appraisal and ensure that the business case includes:

- analysis of the completeness of costs;

- validation/audit of proposed benefits;

- calculation of organization-specific measures of business case value (for example, internal rate of return, net present value of expenditure);

- recommendation to proceed.

Although these constitute a substantial pack of documents, they are a sensible and necessary prerequisite to securing approval to proceed to the product selection and investment appraisal stage, with all the effort and involvement with third parties that this will require.

Each document so far produced will be re-used, developed further or referred back to as the project proceeds, so none of the work will have been wasted.

SUMMARY OF CHAPTER MESSAGES

- The proposed operational model should be defined in order to develop an initial understanding of what the solution will look like, how it is going to work both from a business standpoint and technically, and how it will deliver the required benefits. By comparing the current and proposed operational models, the degree and main focus of change management will become apparent.

- A PID should be produced, which describes what the project aims to achieve, why it is necessary, how it will be delivered, who will do it, when each stage will be done by, and how it will be controlled.

- A fully costed business case should be produced to drive a decision at senior levels on whether the proposed expenditure on HR transformation technology can be justified; whether the project should proceed and to prioritise the planning process.

- It can be advantageous to use third parties to help prepare the business case to ensure it is validated against best practice based on external delivery experience, and that all opportunities have been taken to exploit the planned investment.

- The business case should include hard benefits for example, headcount savings and technology savings, as well as less obvious benefits such as cost avoidance, reduction in third-party costs, opportunity/indirect benefits and service level improvements.

Selecting the Technology

The purpose of this chapter is to describe how an organization should go about choosing the HR technology product(s) which best suit its needs. We will compare various approaches to achieving this, to help you decide which might be most appropriate for your organization.

Assuming that the business case for investment has been approved, the HR project team will now be let loose on the HR systems market with, potentially, a very large sum of money burning a hole in their collective pocket.

The process of selection is frequently a major exercise in its own right, and many organizations can take several months to go through the tasks of articulating requirements to suppliers, attending product demonstrations and constructing elaborate evaluation matrices to compare the relative merits of different products.

The process is highly varied between organizations and may involve a whole range of procurement activity and specialist buying and contract negotiation skills. Certainly, in the public sector, there are strict rules governing procurement, which may offer very limited flexibility over the process for spending large sums of public money.

However, many organizations in non-regulated sectors also apply very stringent demands on the procurement process out of concern to 'choose the right solution'. The net result can be an over-elaborate, complex and time-consuming process that spends a disproportionate amount of time and effort selecting software when, as we have already discussed, this is not the most significant success factor in the project.

Software is not the only commodity likely to be on offer; it is increasingly common for software vendors to 'partner' with the major consultancies offering implementation services as part of a 'total solution'. Project teams may find that their software selection process is inextricably linked to decisions on what external consultancy services to acquire also.

The rapid growth of the systems integration consulting market in recent years has created some unholy alliances. As discussed in Chapter 6, consultant organizations that previously declared their independence in the process, now depend heavily upon the consultancy business derived from the implementation of the two major ERP suppliers (Oracle/PeopleSoft and SAP). To deliver complex systems integration projects, many consultancies maintain teams of consultants dedicated to a particular solution and their own sales teams will work in close alliance with those of the software supplier. A business, therefore, may have no idea that a particular consultancy is working closely with the software supplier who recommended them. Because of this, the value of the truly independent adviser to the project manager and indeed HR may well prove pivotal in ensuring that the best solution is identified to meet the needs of the organization.

In short, there are a number of approaches to selecting HR technology products, involving significant differences in resources, tasks, risk, complexity and timescales. It is, therefore, important to achieve the most cost-effective outcome to this potentially convoluted project stage. The next section discusses three such approaches, which we have termed *traditional*, *accelerated* and *radical.*

Traditional Approach to Product Selection

The traditional approach to selection typically involves publicising the opportunity to bid to as wide a range of suppliers as possible. This approach is often adopted in public sector procurement processes where the need is seen to run an objective process is paramount.

Figure 7.1 sets out the traditional approach to product selection. This approach involves a number of sequential tasks, each of which is briefly described below.

Prepare statement of user requirements:

- package functional requirements (those relating to HR processes)

- package non-functional requirements (those relating to technical requirements, usability and requirements for support etc.)

- implementation requirements.

Prepare evaluation plan; key criteria for evaluation are likely to include:

- functional requirements

- non-functional requirements

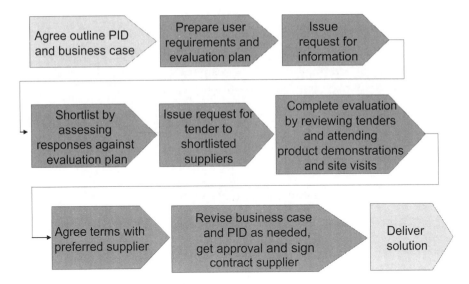

Figure 7.1   Traditional approach to product selection

- supplier profile

- ability to support benefits

- total cost of ownership

- timeline and key steps (see Appendix A for sample requirements documentation contents and solution evaluation plans).

Prepare information pack; likely information will include:

- your own organization profile

- HR structures, deployment, location and so on

- services provided by HR and transaction volumes for the main processes

- high-level costs of the current service

- current technology platform

- summary HR strategy document.

Issue request for information to potential vendors:

- issue information pack

- define scope of service required

- specify financial analysis required from the supplier

- prepare evaluation scorecard aligned to requirements

- specify format in which response is needed (to enable easy comparison with other vendors)

- explain next step in process for vendors, specifically how shortlisting will be carried out.

Assess responses and shortlist:

- modify evaluation matrix if necessary

- nominate evaluation team

- carry out initial review of written responses against evaluation plan

- arrange for vendors to 'present' case to evaluation team

- score vendors individually and consolidate into a single view

- agree recommendation with project lead and or sponsor

- notify shortlisted vendors and offer feedback to those unsuccessful.

Issue request for tender:

- prepare a detailed set of functional requirements

- prepare detailed technical requirements including existing platform

- involve procurement specialists to input contractual requirements

- include high-level plan

- HR Strategy detail

- reinforce description of scope of services plus future service development plans.

Final evaluation:

- invite vendors to present proposal to evaluation team

- thoroughly review proposal and obtain any clarification prior to presentation

- modify evaluation criteria if needed

- prepare common questions for all vendors plus any 'vendor specific'

- score proposals individually for discussion with evaluation team and agree final scores

- evaluation team make recommendations to project team/sponsor for approval

- confirm to successful vendor 'subject to contract' and secure written outline agreement before notifying unsuccessful vendors

- feedback to unsuccessful vendors.

Revise business case:

- update cost and benefit sections

- modify other areas where needed

- ensure project specialists – IT/finance/procurement sign-off

- present to project manager/sponsor for final approval

- secure written approval to proceed.

Sign contract:

- ensure contract is approved by procurement and legal teams

- ensure IT and finance sign off appropriate clauses

- brief organization's signatory to ensure full understanding of content

- project manager ensures that all internal procedures have been followed and approvals granted before arranging for contracts to be signed.

The traditional approach is most appropriate where key stakeholders need convincing that the marketplace has been explored fully and objectively, or where due process requires a wholly democratic approach to shortlisting and selection.

Accelerated Approach to Product Selection

The assumption underpinning this approach is that there are, in reality, only a small number of suitable suppliers who can provide the type of product being sought and it is therefore unnecessary, expensive and time-consuming to invite expressions of interest and/or tenders from a multitude of suppliers. Therefore, this approach (as shown in Figure 7.2) bypasses some of the early stages of the traditional approach by eliminating the request for information and shortlisting stages.

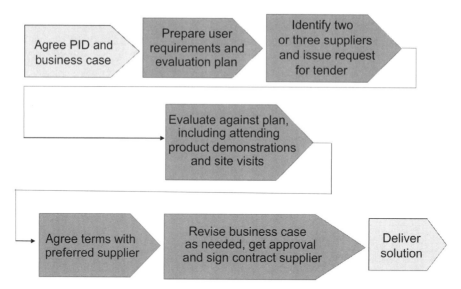

Figure 7.2   Accelerated approach to product selection

Under this approach, which tends to be commonly used in the private sector, one or more overriding factors are identified, which limit the choice of product, for example:

- Is there a limited number of recognized market leaders?

- Does the organization have an existing relationship with any of the suppliers or use any of their other products?

- Does the IT strategy and existing architecture particularly favour one solution over another?

- Does the use of other applications from the same suppliers (for example, use of finance applications or self-service related to other applications) mean that integration with HR will be significantly easier?

- Is there an in-house skill base in one particular product set?

- Do the users have a strong pre-disposition towards one product? (That is, have they decided already?)

Taking the first of these points as an example, an HR systems project of any size is likely to encounter the two giants of the ERP industry, Oracle (which now includes The Oracle and PeopleSoft HR product sets within its stable) and SAP. Both provide a comprehensive range of HR transformation technology software incorporating self-service functionality, reporting capability and close integration with their related suites of products. Both will present a powerful argument as to the capabilities of their products and the benefits that the organization can derive. Both will provide reference sites with directly comparable business issues that will give glowing testament to the quality of the products and services. It is therefore perfectly normal for organizations of a certain size and type to confine the scope of package selection to these two vendors and their products.

By this means, therefore, it is possible to eliminate some 50 per cent of the traditional selection stage. However, this approach can still get heavily bogged down during evaluation (even though there may be only two or three products), since this still involves a plan, a team, product demonstrations and site visits. The final approach, discussed below, simplifies the selection stage further.

Radical Approach to Product Selection

This approach avoids the need for a selection decision, by considering on the product(s) of a single vendor who might be the organization's preferred supplier. This results in a dramatically truncated selection stage as shown in Figure 7.3.

This approach alters the whole structure of project initiation and feasibility because the task of reviewing the preferred package takes place alongside the preparation of the PID and business case, which are based around that product.

The premise underpinning this approach is that too many HR transformation technology projects focus too much attention on the selection phase at the expense of more important areas, even in cases where an accelerated approach is taken. It is not unusual to see selection processes involving combined teams of HR, IT, procurement and business professionals engaged in lengthy software

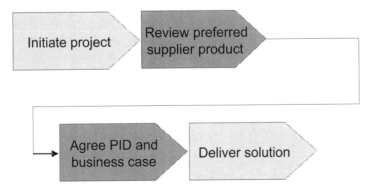

Figure 7.3   Radical approach to product selection

evaluations and programmes of vendor visits that can span several months. One organization spent close to six months evaluating three main software vendors and less than a week selecting a project manager who would carry the responsibility for delivering the project!

The intensive focus on software selection at the expense of other areas is often misguided. The wrong choice of software may sometimes cause a project to fail, but there are numerous other more likely reasons, some of the main ones being:

- unrealistic business case

- unclear project goals

- uncommitted stakeholders

- inadequate project sponsorship

- poor project management.

Whilst products with poor functionality or lack of scalability should be avoided, the clear indication is that the major suppliers' products can be made to work very effectively or can fail very badly in any organization. In view of this, it may be simplest to adopt one of them at the outset and focus the effort on achieving successful delivery. The key to making that decision goes back to the limiting factors which underpin the accelerated approach which, to recap, are:

- Is there a limited number of recognized market leaders?

- Does the organization have an existing relationship with any of the suppliers or use any of their other products?

- Does the IT strategy and existing architecture particularly favour one solution over another?

- Does the use of other applications from the same suppliers (for example, use of finance applications or self-service related to other applications) mean that integration with HR will be significantly easier?

- Is there an in-house skill base in one particular product set?

- Is there a strong pre-disposition from the users to one product (that is, have they decided already)?

Under the radical approach, analysis of these factors will generally point to a clear winner, rather than having two or three favourites. In this case it would certainly still be important to demonstrate that the preferred solution can do the job required of it and the project team may not escape the need to attend product demonstrations, make reference visits and evaluate the solution against their requirements. However, if the preferred package is identified early, the project loses the overhead of having to evaluate and compare different applications.

Clearly there is also the question of how to ensure a supplier provides a competitive price, particularly if they are labelled early as the preferred supplier. In the event of a 'radical' selection process, the price should reflect the opportunity for the supplier to avoid the cost and effort involved in participating in a competitive sales process requiring responses to tender documents, demonstrations and client visits, which can amount to a significant 'cost of sale' for them. Given the opportunity to have a 'clear run' at a client's requirements without any direct competition, most will be very willing to consider highly competitive pricing. This can be checked against pricing estimates received in the business case phase as well as previous quotes or actual costs for other applications in use across the organization. Should the supplier fail to take advantage of their opportunity then the organization will have lost nothing, as they will still be free to approach other suppliers at a later date.

The obvious benefit of this approach is that it saves time money and resources. As stated above, certain processes need to be gone through to demonstrate due diligence. This can be reinforced and made even more cost-effective by engaging an independent HR transformation partner to validate and, if required, manage this approach.

SUMMARY OF CHAPTER MESSAGES

- The traditional approach to supplier selection involves publicizing the opportunity to bid to as wide a range of suppliers as possible. This is most appropriate where key stakeholders need convincing that the marketplace has been explored fully and objectively, or where due process requires a wholly democratic approach to attracting and shortlisting suppliers.

- The accelerated approach to supplier selection assumes is that there are, in reality, only a small number of suitable suppliers who can provide the type of product being sought and it is therefore unnecessary, expensive and time-consuming to invite expressions of interest and/or tenders from a multitude of suppliers. Therefore, this approach bypasses some of the early stages of the traditional approach by eliminating the request for information and shortlisting stages.

- In the radical approach to supplier selection, the main focus is on validating the capability of an organization's preferred supplier to deliver the required solution. Thus, the task of reviewing the preferred package takes place alongside the preparation of the PID and business case, which are based around that product. The premise underpinning this approach is that too many HR transformation technology projects focus too much attention on the selection phase at the expense of more important areas, even in cases where an accelerated approach is taken.

Delivering HR Technology

This chapter describes the tasks involved in implementing the chosen HR transformation technology solution(s). This is normally the longest, most complex and risky stage in any HR transformation technology project, and is usually managed in four broad phases as follows:

- design phase

- build phase

- test phase

- rollout phase.

The whole stage should be managed under tight day-to-day project controls, which we will describe firstly, before going on to cover the phases shown above.

Project Control

Project managers have at their disposal a number of mechanisms for controlling project delivery. These should be used appropriately, to achieve a balance that allows effective project management without enmeshing the project team in layers of bureaucracy that places form-filling above project delivery. Some of the more commonly used techniques are described below.

RISK MANAGEMENT

This involves logging key risks, including an assessment of their potential impact and probability of occuring or controllability. Mitigating actions can then be identified and progress monitored, with the aim of preventing them becoming issues requiring urgent attention. The risk log should be kept up to date and monitored regularly to ensure risks are being managed appropriately (see Appendix A for sample risk/issue log).

ISSUE MANAGEMENT

If, despite risk management, issues do arise, they need to be logged and assessed for impact, and mitigating actions identified so that they can be managed. As in the case of risks, the issue log should be subject to regular review and update, to ensure that issues are not allowed to rumble on, and are closed out comprehensively and speedily.

PROGRESS REPORTING

Regular reporting is needed at programme, project and workstream level, to ensure that a balanced view of progress can be ascertained and communicated, and that major issues are visible and can be addressed. In a large project, the project manager may call for weekly written reports from each workstream lead in his or her management team, who will then meet to review progress. From this, a consolidated report can be prepared by the project manager for the project board and/or programme management. It is common to assess workstream, project and programme status in terms of R (red), A (amber) G (green):

- Red – project off track with no plan in place to bring it back on track.

- Amber – off track but with a plan in place to bring back on track.

- Green – on track.

This provides an at a glance view of overall status and is a valuable tool for communicating progress to management, project team and other stakeholders (see Appendix A for sample progress report).

PLAN MONITORING

Detailed project or workstream plans may be maintained within a specialist project management package (for example, MS Project). This allows each task involved in project delivery to be recorded, along with their 'baselined' start and end dates, associated resource and dependencies. Tasks can be grouped for clarity, according to milestones, and the data displayed in various formats, most usually Gantt charts, providing a graphic view of how the plan hangs together, its critical path and resource profile. As the project proceeds, revised forecast dates can be entered so that the plan can highlight any delays and discrepancies against the baseline version.

BENEFITS TRACKING AND BUDGET MONITORING

The business case spreadsheet should be updated regularly with actual figures and revised forecasts in the form of monthly costs and benefits, and changes in anticipated spend and savings. Detailed costs can be recorded using the general ledger, if suitable, or a more detailed spreadsheet. Monthly reports should be produced, showing actual to-date figures and forecast costs and benefits, so that remedial action can be taken in good time.

QUALITY CONTROL

Performance against the quality plan (see Chapter 6) should also be monitored, to ensure that delivery is to the required standard. Quality criteria should be associated with key deliverables, and it is important to ensure that time is built in for quality reviews, with results logged. 'Gate', 'exit/entry' or 'go/no-go' criteria should be defined as a basis for assessing whether it is appropriate to proceed to the next stage or key phase, and these should include quality criteria for key deliverables, for example, specifications, configuration, testing, training and so on.

CHANGE CONTROL

As the project proceeds, it is likely that new requirements will emerge or that issues will force a different approach to delivery; for example, it may prove necessary to customize the package because its functionality proves to be insufficient. These things shouldn't happen, but they do, and a formal process is required to ensure that major changes are managed to avoid scope drift and consequent overruns on plan and budget. Change control requires that all impacts of proposed changes to scope or approach are assessed in terms of cost, timing and impacts across the project. For example, a major change to system design will not only have implications for configuration, but may also have an impact on related systems, interfaces and conversion programs, as well as on other workstreams; for example, testing, training and implementation.

As delivery proceeds and pressures increase, it usually becomes necessary to tighten change control by introducing two further measures:

- 'technical' change control, whereby *all* changes, even minor configuration adjustments, need to be assessed for their impact on the project by relevant parties; for example, training, or end users;

- 'pre'-change control, whereby all change requests are vetted before formal impact assessment is carried out. This weeds out any 'non-starters' that are not worthy of further investigation, given that impact assessment itself imposes demands on severely stretched resources.

With the above disciplines in place and running effectively, let us now examine the phases involved in delivering the chosen solution and completing the project.

Approaches to Design and Build

The preceding stages should have delivered a sound platform for the design and build phase in the form of:

- agreed project vision, scope and objectives

- agreed business design principles (for example, standardization – see Chapter 6)

- high-level business process requirements

- high-level interface and MI requirements

- a procured solution, based on a systematic selection process which has demonstrated quite specifically how the package(s) can fulfil your business requirements.

Before commencing design and build, it is important to understand how approaches may differ, depending on factors such as the type of product being implemented, the extent to which requirements are standard and the knowledge and skills of the users. These points are explored further in the following sections.

CONFIGURATION VERSUS CUSTOMIZATION

As stated earlier, the main reason for choosing a package rather than attempting to develop a solution from scratch is that today's HR software normally includes a ready-made set of workflow and processing tools and templates. As such, these packages are configurable: that is they can be adapted easily to fit a customer's business processes without needing to change the system's 'source code', that is, the more complex computer programs on which the package is built.

It is therefore highly desirable that business requirements remain within the limits of the system's configurability. This avoids customization, which (a) requires all the rigour of programming discussed in the previous paragraph, (b) will not be supported by the supplier and (c) may cease to work when the supplier releases periodic upgrades to its software. Therefore project managers should think very carefully before recommending to their project boards that any HR package should be customized. It may be simpler to change the organization's business processes – after all, the better packages will have been built on best practice foundations.

One compromise approach offered by some package suppliers is for non-standard code to be allowed to be developed by the customer organization at recognized places in the package structure. This at least controls the exit and re-entry points of 'enhancements' that the supplier will not support, enabling them to maintain a clean line between what is covered, and not covered, by future product upgrades.

THE TRADITIONAL APPROACH – DEVELOPMENT

Figure 8.1 shows the route map through 'traditional' system design and build, as applies when systems are developed from scratch by programmers rather than by the configuration of packages.

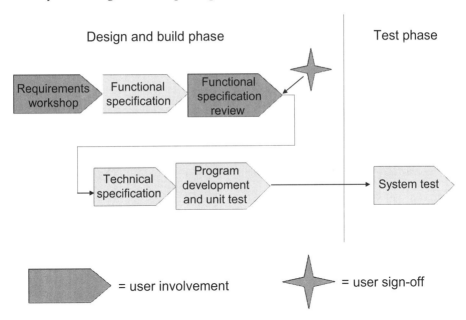

Figure 8.1   Traditional approach to design and build

In today's world, this approach is rarely, if ever, taken to the building of entire HR systems (for example, payroll, HR, CRM). However, it does apply to quite a lot of what goes on around the edges of solution design and build in what is often termed 'RICE':

- *reports*: the bespoking of specific reports which cannot be delivered within the standard package;

- *interfaces*: from the new solution to existing related systems, or indeed between different components of the new solution if products supplied by different vendors are used;

- *conversion programs*: for migrating data from the systems being replaced ('legacy' systems) into the new solution; and

- *enhancements*: where customization proves to be unavoidable.

This approach is characterized by:

- *Longer lead times*: Programs typically take longer to specify and build than package configuration, because they use less powerful computer languages. They are also far harder to amend when errors or changes to requirements occur.

- *Less user involvement*: users tend to have only two inputs during the design and build stage in the traditional development route, firstly when preparing initial requirements and again when reviewing functional specification.

The traditional approach therefore carries more risk, in terms of timescale and quality.

THE ACCELERATED APPROACH – CONFIGURATION

The accelerated approach, which applies to package configuration, is shown in Figure 8.2.

This approach is characterized by greater user involvement during the design and build stage and, despite the apparently greater number of steps involved, faster delivery times. This is because configuration involves the use of more powerful and flexible tools, which allow solutions to be built more speedily and changed more easily. This is not an excuse for users to be slapdash when specifying requirements, but it does mean that they can see and influence the solution at various key points during the design and build.

The accelerated approach takes various guises; for example, rapid application development (RAD) or joint application development (JAD). Taken to their logical extremes, these approaches can involve users, business analysts and configurers being locked in a room for however long it takes to accomplish the entire design and build phase in one hit.

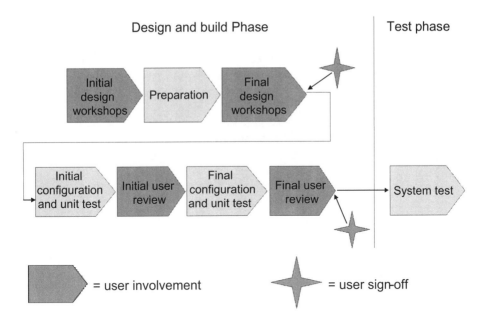

Figure 8.2   Accelerated approach to design and build

The Design Phase

DESIGN DELIVERABLES

Business Process Maps

Business processes are usually documented in the form of a process design pack, comprising:

- a top-level map covering the entire business process scope of the project;

- for each process area, second-level and below maps until all the main steps are captured, both IT and non-IT steps; that is, full end-to-end processes; and

- detailed descriptions of each work procedure containing work instructions and layouts for standard letters, reports, e-mails and so on. In the case of a HR CRM system, these would include script flows governing the route of the conversation between an HR SSC agent and a customer, and knowledge management content and indexing requirements.

Figure 8.3 shows how one process from a top-level map can be 'decomposed' into second-level processes, including a task that can be opened out to highlight some of its detailed work procedures.

The process design pack is the glue which binds together the solution design. It shows:

- which tasks have to be carried out

- who does them

- where they are done

- how they are done

- how work flows between them

- which tasks are automated and which are manual

- which hand-offs are manual and which are via an interface

- which processes and tasks are in scope.

As covered in Chapter 6, a high-level cut of the process design may have been initiated during the preparation of the business model proposed as part of the project initiation/feasibility stage, and then developed further during the product selection stage. Given that packages come with pre-defined processes, this should involve aligning the organization's business processes to those supplied within the package, so that the solution can be built by configuration rather than customization.

DATA AND DATA CONVERSION DEFINITIONS

Alongside business process documentation, it is necessary to define the data items that these processes will use. The information required will include:

- A data model, showing how the main groups of data (or 'entities', for example, employee data, organizational data, training data and so on) are related. As with the business processes, this structure should be governed by the package, with any additional or changed fields handled by configuration rather than customization.

- Fields, by screen (again, based on what is supplied as standard by the package), showing field titles, lengths, validation and so on.

- Codes, where fields allow a defined range of possible entries (for example, sickness codes).

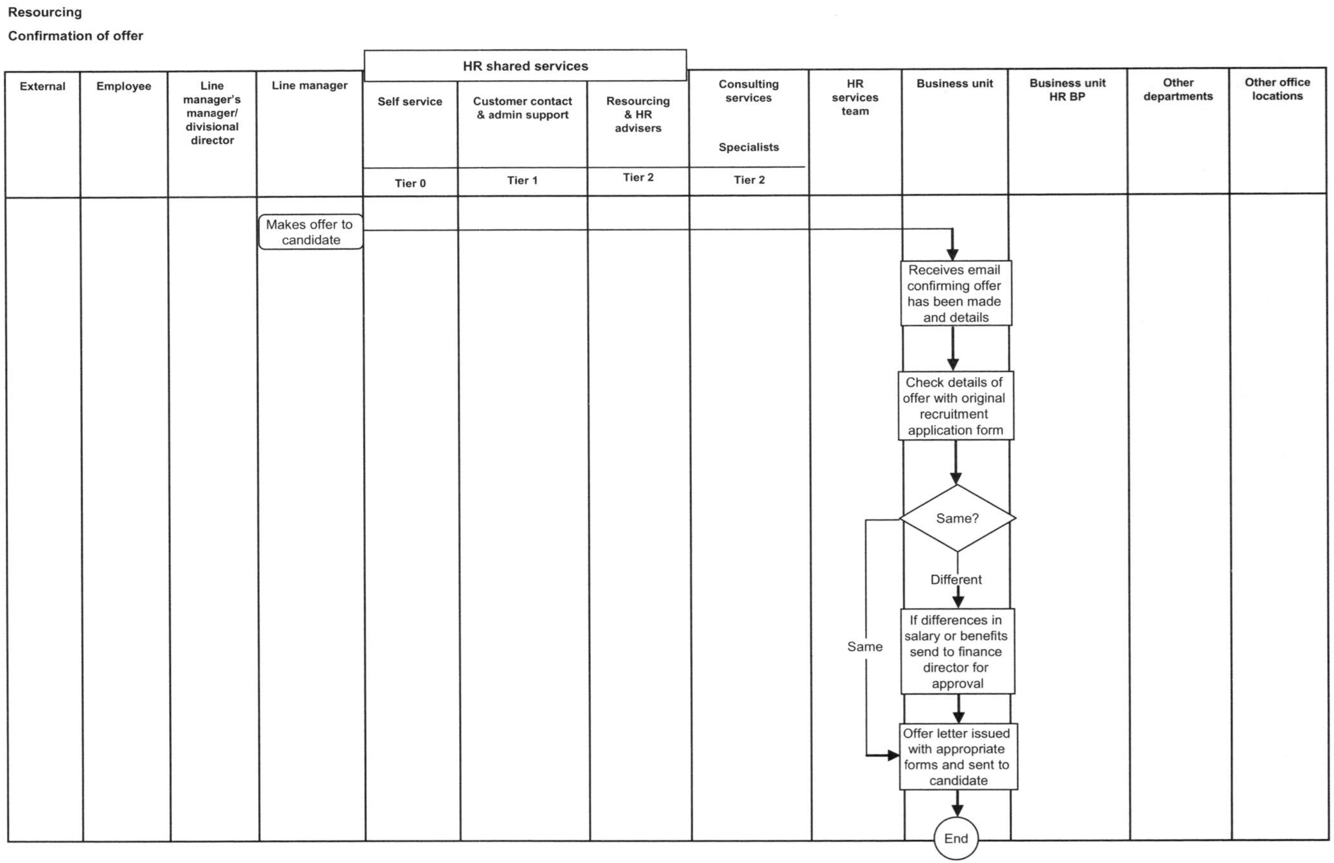

Resourcing
Confirmation of offer

External	Employee	Line manager's manager/ divisional director	Line manager	HR shared services			Consulting services	HR services team	Business unit	Business unit HR BP	Other departments	Other office locations
				Self service	Customer contact & admin support	Resourcing & HR advisers	Specialists					
				Tier 0	Tier 1	Tier 2	Tier 2					

Line manager: Makes offer to candidate

Business unit:
- Receives email confirming offer has been made and details
- Check details of offer with original recruitment application form
- Same? → Different / Same
- If differences in salary or benefits send to finance director for approval
- Offer letter issued with appropriate forms and sent to candidate
- End

Figure 8.3   Process design process

- If a current or 'legacy' system is being replaced, a table that maps the old system's fields to the new, including conversion rules. This ensures that nothing important from the legacy system is being ignored and provides the basis for the data conversion program that will need to be developed if data are being transferred automatically from the old to the new systems.

- Definition of any historical data that is being brought over from the old to the new system. These data, which will be transferred by the conversion programme, might include a number of years' payroll, salary, employment, performance, training or sickness data.

'STRUCTURAL' FUNCTIONALITY DEFINITIONS

Many packages are built around critical 'structural' functionality, which forms the backbone of the new solution. If these are designed incorrectly, the solution will be flawed and the ramifications of this will be felt throughout the remainder of the project and beyond. Three HR transformation technology examples of these structural requirements are given below:

1. The organization management (OM) structure in an HR system

The OM structure in an HR system describes how the organization is divided into business areas and functions, and, within these, how jobs and positions are defined and related to each other. Employees are linked to the organization structure by their position, and this relationship is used by the system to reflect a range of personnel attributes, for example:

- their terms and conditions, governed by the type of job they do, or the area in which they work;

- their learning and development needs, which can be driven by comparing the requirements of the job with the attributes of the individual; and

- their usage of the system – what information they are allowed to see and use, and how it is processed (for example, to whom their requests for leave are forwarded).

2. The business model in an ERP system

Where the scope of a system transcends functional boundaries (for example, HR, finance and procurement), the way in which the business is represented within the system controls how effectively the solution will meet the organization's needs. This governs the representation of important entities such as:

- the charter of accounts

- the legal company structure

- HR groupings

- payroll groupings

- the organization.

3. The work categorization list in an HR CRM system

The categorization of work is core to an HR CMS and may govern:

- how work is allocated

- how work is actioned and tracked

- how work is analyzed and reported on.

MANAGEMENT INFORMATION REQUIREMENTS DEFINITION

The use of flexible ad hoc reporting tools or 'data warehouse' solutions should reduce the need for full MI requirements specification. However, the composition of any data groupings, queries or 'cubes' will need to be defined to ensure that data can be reported upon in the required combination. It is also important to define how reports might be limited, sorted, scheduled, run and distributed.

If customized reports do prove to be necessary, full specifications will be needed.

INTERFACE REQUIREMENTS DEFINITION

A variety of interfaces may be needed between the various HR technology solutions (for example, CMS, HR/Payroll system, telephony, document imaging and so on). Business or functional specifications for these interfaces must be prepared for review alongside the process design pack.

The functional specifications for interfaces will need to describe:

- business volumes;

- the required frequency of the interfaces (monthly, daily, hourly and so on);

- mapping requirements for data being passed from the sending system to its equivalent in the receiving system.

They will form a basis for the technical interface specifications, which will be written early in the build phase by the programmers as a basis for the interfaces to be developed.

SECURITY AND ACCESS REQUIREMENTS DEFINITION

While processes are being designed, it is important to identify who will carry out each task within each process. This will highlight which system roles are needed, and how they can be matched to users' jobs, so that user profiles can be designed. As a rule, the simpler the security requirements, the easier the design and the less the potential impact on system performance.

This task may form part of a wider business change initiative, involving major changes to HR roles. It may also sit within a wider system security exercise, which reviews the new end-to-end processes and the system environment to ensure that the new operational model conforms to the organization's security standards. This may involve internal audit, whose role as one of the key stakeholders in an HR technology project should have been recognized during start up/feasibility (see Chapter 4).

KNOWLEDGE MANAGEMENT (KM) REQUIREMENTS DEFINITION (CMS)

During the design phase of an HR CRM system, it is important to identify KM requirements in terms of:

- *Content*: Which documents will be used, and will any new ones need to be originated; for example, frequently asked questions (FAQs)?

- *Format*: Does the package require a particular format for example, Word, PDF or HTML?

- *Indexing*: How should the KM content be indexed to deliver optimal trade-off between ease of indexing and content accessibility?

The Design Process

DESIGN WORKSHOPS

The design of the chosen solution is usually developed by conducting a series of workshops, involving several parties:

- *Users*, who can articulate the requirements in business terms;

- *Business analysts*, who can lead the workshops and translate the user requirements into system language;

- *Configurers*, who are skilled in the use of the chosen package, and will go on to to build the system.

It is absolutely vital that all key stakeholders are represented at the workshops, and that they have empowered their representatives to make decisions during the sessions. If this does not happen, the workshops will falter whilst in session because key design decisions cannot be reached, or the process will stumble after the workshops if previous agreements have to be unpicked because of subsequent contradictory input from key stakeholders.

Workshops can be quite intense affairs, since their aim is to chisel out the precise 'to be' solution while all the key people are in the room together. As the day unfolds, the walls become covered with process maps and lists of issues and actions. By the end of the session, the processes should have been largely mapped out, with only relatively minor tasks outstanding, for example, gathering detailed codes or additional report layouts. If this degree of definition has not been achieved at the workshop, it will be difficult to tie up the loose ends within the timescales required by the project plan. Hence the criticality of securing HR SMEs to ensure requirements are fully fleshed out – otherwise problems at test and implementation will be costly and time-consuming to correct.

As stated above, in the case of a package approach, solution design should reflect the package's modules, and it is usually sensible for the workshop programme to reflect this structure. For example, in an HR system project, workstreams are likely to be required for reward, payroll, employee relations, resourcing, learning and development, employee administration, OM, MI, interfaces, security and access and data conversion. In the case of an HR CRM project, additional workshops may be required for generic processes (for example, ID&V) and KM.

INITIAL WORKSHOPS

Initial workshops should be held for each of the design workstreams. The purpose of these workshops is for the users, facilitated by the business analysts, to communicate the system requirements to the configurers down a fine level of detail, so that the configurers can take away a clear idea of how they are going to build the system.

The users should bring with them to the workshop a set of preparatory material (for example, policy manuals), report layouts, standard letters and e-mails, scripts (CRM), current system process flowcharts (particularly where the required solution is likely to be similar), code lists (for example, absence) and so on. These documents can be referred to and used during the workshops, or taken away by the configurers.

The configurers should, from their knowledge of how the system works, suggest how specific requirements might be fulfilled, so that any system-driven constraints can be discussed and worked through. By the end of the workshop the configurers should have a detailed understanding of the business requirement and how they plan to configure the package to meet it. After the workshop, the configurer or analyst should issue a record of the meeting, including actions outstanding.

INTER-WORKSHOP PREPARATION

Following the initial workshops, the business analysts will prepare an integrated solution design document pack, including:

- process maps
- process descriptions
- procedures
- forms and letters
- scriptflows, and KM specifications (CRM system)
- screen layouts
- field definitions
- functional specifications for interfaces and conversion programs.

If practical, it can be useful to prepare a prototype of the solution, based on the emergent design, for review at the follow-up workshop. A prototype is nothing more than a high-level façade of the solution, requiring minimal configuration, which can be thrown away after use. It is in no sense a comprehensive, fully tested or quality-assured version of the solution, although if done cleverly, it can be made to look like one. The advantage of a prototype is that it brings to life the somewhat thick and dusty book of design documentation by showing users how their solution will look and feel, and how their inputs have been reflected in system design.

FOLLOW-UP WORKSHOPS

After a short period following each initial workshop (typically 2–4 weeks), follow-up workshops should be held, repeating the structure used for the initial set of workshops. The purpose of the follow-up workshops is for the users to review the design documentation (and the prototype, if applicable) prepared by the project team.

If the workshop proceeds without major hitches, it may be possible for the users to sign off the documentation at the end of the workshop. More typically, there will be outstanding actions from the workshop (for example, issues to be resolved, documents to be amended), and the project team will need to confirm when these are complete. If the unresolved issues are significant, a further workshop may be needed following a short period of re-design.

Other Work Needed During System Design

The last days or weeks of the design phase tend to be highly pressurized, with decisions on a range of outstanding issues being finalized and documented. However, if time is not to be lost on the project's critical path, the tasks of other major workstreams need to be advanced in parallel with design, as discussed below.

TEST STRATEGY

The outline test approach set out in the PID needs to be fleshed out into a testing strategy, so that detailed planning can commence in a timely manner. The strategy should address issues such as:

- Approach: verification (that the system has been 'built right') and validation (that the right system has been built).

- Scope: for example, unit testing (normally part of build), system and integration testing, performance testing, regression testing, user acceptance testing and so on.

- Who will be involved in each type of test?

- Where will each type of test take place; what facilities are needed?

- When will they take place – what window is earmarked for each test?

- How will testing be conducted (fault tracking tool, environment requirements, whether to use real data, and whether data should be anonymized)?

- In the case of payroll testing, an approach to parallel running should be provided.

- Time – allow sufficient time to complete testing, since experience tells us that many projects running behind schedule often reduce the time allowed for testing, sharply raising the risk of problems at implementation.

TRAINING STRATEGY

Similarly, the outline training approach set out in the PID must be developed into a training strategy, so that this detailed planning can also commence in a timely manner. The strategy should address issues such as:

- training needs analysis – the types of roles requiring training, and what their occupants need to be trained in given the nature of the new solution and what they have done to date;

- the types of training methods to be used; for example, CBT, classroom-based;

- the location and facilities required; for example, dedicated training room, PCs and so on;

- rough estimates of numbers to be trained;

- an outline of training content.

IMPLEMENTATION PLANNING

Also drawing on the PID, implementation planning should be developed, for example:

- to identifying the Pilot site (if applicable);

- to agree a phasing order for system roll-out;

- to define key cutover activities and dependencies.

TECHNICAL MODEL

The technical model developed during the initiation/feasibility stage should be refined to reflect the chosen package and design, for example:

- precise hardware needs, based on more accurate transaction volumes;

- environment requirements and when needed; for example, for testing and training;

- precise software requirements, including relevant version or release details, patch numbers and so on;

- database requirements;

- storage requirements.

Signing-off the Design

After the workshops are complete, the documentation should be finalized and issued to key stakeholders for sign-off. Whilst this should not be a mere formality, it should be fairly straightforward if the right people participated in the workshops.

The key deliverable at the end of the design phase is detailed design documentation, often termed a system 'blueprint'. This will consist of all the process documents and other types of definition statements described earlier in this section. It serves two main purposes:

- it describes the solution with sufficient precision to show the business that it is what they require and permit sign-off;

- it is sufficiently detailed for the configurers' purposes so that they can build the solution.

If no major problems are anticipated but there is likely to be a delay in getting sign-off, it may be valid with project board agreement to commence the building of the solution 'at risk', rather than holding everything up for several weeks while sign-off is obtained.

Building the Solution

PACKAGE CONFIGURATION

Whilst there will be the need to develop interfaces, conversion programs plus the occasional enhancement, the build phase should largely focus on package configuration, which can be done relatively speedily provided the blueprint is comprehensive and signed off. Because of this, it is possible to allow users one or two opportunities to confirm that the solution being built matches what they have signed off, and the process is often structured as follows:

1.   *Initial configuration*: most (approximately 80 per cent) configuration is undertaken – this should include any structural configuration (for example, OM, business model, CRM work classification list), and the majority of the simpler configuration. This will have been unit tested by (other) configurers against the design blueprint to eliminate any avoidable errors ahead of review by users.

2.   *Initial validation*: an optional albeit desirable interim review by the users of the 80 per cent solution. This may result in minor adjustments to the configuration, which can be accommodated by the project without change control.

3.   *Final configuration*: the remaining configuration, including any agreed adjustments arising from any initial confirmation, and unit testing.

4.   *Final validation*: final review by users, and sign-off.

DEVELOPMENT

This covers any non-standard build (that is, additional to configuration); for example, interfaces, conversion programs, enhancements, non-standard reports or forms. Taking interfaces as an example, the first task is to translate the functional specifications into technical specifications as a basis for developing the computer programs. This is good discipline even where the specifications and the programs are developed by the same team. If the programs are written offshore, clear and well-written specifications are especially important in order to avoid costly and time-consuming errors and re-work. The specifications will need to address:

*   Whether the interface is real time (using 'web services' technology) or more traditional batch programming. Factors to balance here include the benefits of immediate data transfer offered by web services versus the additional risk and possible complexity of this approach, for example in error handling (see last bullet below).

*   How frequently any batch programs should be run. For example it may be sufficient to update an HR CRM with core personal details from the HR system on a daily basis.

- Precise mapping requirements, between the system generating the interface (outbound) and the receiving system (inbound), and any processing needed to achieve this.

- How errors should be handled, which can be particularly complex when data are moving between two major HR systems; for example, overtime entered via the CRM system being interfaced through to the HR/payroll system.

As stated earlier, interface development is a less transparent process than package configuration and it is unlikely that users will be able to see a fully working interface program ahead of the formal testing stage. However, it should be possible for the configurers to provide mock-ups of interfaces at confirmation workshops so that their fit with the configured processes can be observed. This, together with inspection of unit test logs by IT project representatives, may have to suffice by way of sign-off that interface and other developments have been concluded successfully ahead of formal system testing.

Other Tasks to be Undertaken During the Build Phase

While the main focus of the build phase will be on configuration and development, progress also needs to be made in other areas in readiness for subsequent phases. These are covered below.

DATA COLLECTION

If a significant quantity of data has to be gathered manually, planning for this should be underway. Examples might include:

- organization data, in the case of a new HR system which involves using OM data for the first time;

- e-mail addresses, for example where a CRM system is being introduced which will require e-mails to be generated by the system's workflow functionality if tasks fall overdue;

- annual leave entitlement, if the new solution will replace myriad local systems for recording this.

DATA CLEANSE

HR data should be maintained accurately as a matter of principle and law, so all organizations should have ongoing procedures in place to achieve this. From a project standpoint, certain types of data have to be 'valid' for the new solution to be able to process them. For example, the project may be less concerned about whether an employee's street number is correct (although it is clearly desirable) than whether the address contains a valid postcode, which may be a mandatory field; if it is not valid the record may fail to load into the new system.

Consequently, the project should liaise with the current ('legacy') system owners to provide reports from these systems highlighting invalid data, which can then be issued to legacy system users for correction.

KNOWLEDGE MANAGEMENT

The design phase should have identified the documents, including FAQs, which will form the KM knowledge base, together with formatting and indexing requirements. These documents should now be gathered, (re)formatted and indexed so that they are ready for testing along with the rest of solution build.

DOCUMENTATION

The most detailed level of process documentation, that is, work procedures, needs to be completed during the build phase, for example by including and documenting screen shots The completed procedures should then be fed into the preparation of test scripts, user guides and training content.

TEST PREPARATION

It is important that system testing should be ready to commence as soon as the design/build phase has been signed off. Therefore, based on the agreed test strategy, the following tasks need to be addressed while the system is being built:

- the test manager and system testing team should have been recruited and trained;

- the technical environment should have been readied for testing (servers, connectivity, PCs with suitable access rights and so on);

- a system test plan and specification should have been prepared and agreed;

- a system test scripts/scenarios should have been prepared utilizing SMEs;

- system test data should have been created;

- a test problem report logging system and procedure should have been implemented;

- acceptance criteria for the system test should have been agreed (for example, zero critical faults outstanding, maximum of 10 non-critical faults outstanding and so on).

TRAINING PREPARATION

Based on the training strategy, detailed preparation for training should be progressing by this stage:

- the training needs analysis should have been signed off

- preparation of course material should be well advanced, including screen shots

- the training environment should be under development

- training facilities should have been procured and kitted out.

COMMUNICATIONS AND BUSINESS CHANGE

Customers should by now have been given initial notification of any major changes to the service arising from the project, and any initial briefings for local management should have been held.

The initial impact analysis of changes brought about by the project should be finalized, now that the complete design has been agreed and documented.

Getting Formal Sign-off to the Build Phase

The project manager should present the project board with a report summarizing progress with the key deliverables from the design/build phase, and updating the PID and business case. The report should confirm that:

- all process build has been signed off by the users;

- interfaces, non-standard reports and forms, and any enhancements have been developed and unit tested;

- any conversion programs have been developed and unit tested;

- all system design documentation is complete;

- training preparation is on track;

- progress against the communications and business change plans is on track;

- preparation for system testing is complete.

If the project board is happy to approve this report, together with any impact on the PID and business case, the build stage may be signed off and testing may now commence.

Test Phase

Testing normally involves two major tasks:

- system testing – to ensure the solution works as specified, including the process configuration, interfaces and other components such as security and MI;

- user acceptance testing (UAT) – to ensure that the solution successfully supports the end-to-end business processes.

In the case of a payroll project, UAT should include one or more parallel runs.

SYSTEM TESTING

The system test involves testing the solution by running test scenarios using pre-written test scripts, the results of which can be compared with pre-defined 'expected' outcomes. The test should be based on design documents (for example, process maps), data definitions, functional specifications and detailed work procedures. Its purpose is to identify where the system is not working, so that errors or 'bugs' can be corrected and re-tested before it is released for user acceptance testing. As such, it is a fairly mechanistic process which is normally carried out by the solution-delivery side of the project team – either by the suppliers/implementation partners themselves, or by a testing team resourced from within the client IT organization (or by a combination of these).

It may be politic to invite the users to observe or even execute some of the system test to maintain openness and business confidence in the project (this is often insisted upon in payroll projects for very good reasons). However, some organizations may judge this to be unnecessary since users will have only recently seen large parts of the system in operation at final confirmation sessions, and will subsequently have the opportunity to test the system fully in the user acceptance test.

System Test Components

The system test specification should describe precisely how each system feature is to be tested, including critical success factors, and should include the following:

- business processes and procedures, including any enhancements;

- management information reports;

- interfaces, including error handling;

- conversion programs (if any);

- security and access – to ensure that users cannot view or update data that they are not authorized to access.

Conducting the System Test

The system test plan should indicate, to a reasonable level of detail, which tests are to be conducted on which days, and the resources required to perform them. This allows progress to be monitored and additional resources to be applied if the test starts to fall behind schedule.

The testers will then work through each test scenario and script, logging precise details of any fault or issue onto the test problem reporting (TPR) system. The status of the TPR log will be monitored by the testing manager, who will allocate faults or 'bugs' back to appropriate configurers or developers for investigation and resolution. The process should allow TPRs to be prioritized and where appropriate cross-referenced to ensure that related bugs are fixed by the same resource. When the fault has been fixed, the test manager will arrange for the test to be re-run.

System testing can generate a huge number of TPRs of varying degrees of complexity, and it is important that the testing and project managers maintain a clear sight of overall progress against plan to ensure that additional resources can be allocated and priorities changed if needed. The project manager should provide the project board with regular summaries of tests completed and key faults and issues logged, so that stakeholders are kept informed of overall system test progress.

Signing off the System Test

It is unlikely that all TPRs will have been resolved by the end of the system test period. However, it is vital that all tests have been conducted within the required timeframe and that the outcome is acceptable; for example, the outstanding TPR count is within the tolerances laid down by the system test acceptance criteria.

At the end of the system test a report should be presented by the project manager to the project board, describing performance against plan and acceptance criteria, and summarizing the outstanding TPRs and when it is proposed to fix them. Based on this report, the project board will decide whether the system is sufficiently robust for it to be made available for UAT.

At the same time, the project board will need to be satisfied that preparation for the UAT has been concluded. Many of the system test resources and facilities can be re-used (for example, the test manager, the TPR system, the acceptance criteria). However, the UAT is not merely a re-run of the system test so the following UAT-specific preparation is necessary:

- The UAT team should be available and trained in how to use each of the technology solutions, at least in their 'vanilla' form; that is, as purchased.

- The UAT technical environment should have been readied for testing (servers, connectivity, PCs with suitable access rights and so on).

- A UAT plan and detailed specification should have been agreed.

- UAT scripts/scenarios should have been prepared.

- UAT data should have been created.

If the project board is satisfied that the system test has been concluded satisfactorily and UAT preparation is complete, it will then grant authorization for the UAT to commence.

USER ACCEPTANCE TESTING (UAT)

The purpose of the UAT is to test the relevant business processes from end to end, in order to ensure that the solution operates satisfactorily and supports the business requirement. The UAT should be carried out by business people who will go on to be actual users of the solution, plus business representatives who were involved in agreeing the requirements and/or design.

Conducting the UAT

As with the system test, the UAT plan should include a schedule indicating which tests are to be performed on which days, and by whom. The testers will then work through the UAT scenarios and scripts, logging precise details of any fault or issue onto the TPR system. The TPR log will be monitored by the testing manager, who will allocate technology faults for investigation, resolution and re-retesting. As with the system test, the project manager must retain a clear overview of overall progress against plan to ensure that additional resources can be allocated and priorities changed if needed (see Appendix A for an example of a test progress summary report).

In the case of the UAT it may be that what appear to the users to be faults are in fact change requests that is, the system performs as specified but does not support the end-to-end business process. In that case an impact assessment of the change will need to be carried out by the project team and agreement reached on the required action. If a major change is needed ahead of go-live, this may need to be cleared with the project board.

As with the system test, it is unlikely that all TPRs will have been resolved by the end of the UAT period. However, it is vital that all tests have been conducted within the required timeframe and that the outstanding TPR count is within the tolerances laid down by the UAT acceptance criteria.

At the end of the UAT a report should be prepared, describing performance against plan and acceptance criteria, and summarizing the outstanding TPRs and when it is proposed to fix them.

Payroll Parallel Runs

In a project which includes payroll, a key aspect of UAT is the parallel run, the scope of which may be defined as:

- testing that the gross to net (GTN) program within the new system generates the same calculated results (gross pay, net pay, deductions, employer's National Insurance/pension contributions and so on) as those generated by the existing ('legacy') system, or that any variances are within acceptable tolerance levels;

- testing that outputs, for example BACS, payslips, postings to ERP general ledgers, interfaces, reports are correct.

Parallel run testing involves giving increasing levels of confidence to payroll management and users that the new system will achieve the above aims. Consequently, a progressive approach is often adopted, for example:

1. a 'pre-parallel run' using a small sample of data, carried out during the early part of UAT to demonstrate that the execution of the gross to net run and the resultant outputs can be executed correctly, as part of end-to-end payroll process testing;

2. a first realistic parallel run, running the new payroll on the complete population (or highly representative sample thereof) and comparing results with the legacy solution;

3. a second parallel run using the following month's data to demonstrate that the new system can cope with typical changes occurring within a payroll month, and can calculate increases to cumulative values correctly;

4. (optionally) a third/final parallel run, maybe on the full population if this hasn't previously been attempted.

The need to carry out parallel runs may considerably extend the testing phase, and this should have been factored into the project plan when the testing approach was first being formulated during initiation/feasibility.

OTHER TYPES OF TESTING

Other, often more technical, testing will also be required alongside functional system testing and user acceptance testing:

1. performance and volume testing – to ensure that the hardware is capable of supporting the required numbers of users, transactions and data volumes, at peak as well as normal loadings;

2. destruction testing, to try to 'crash' the system for example, by hitting irrelevant keys;

3. technical features, for example, how the system copes with hardware or database failure partway through a transaction;

4. regression testing, to demonstrate that the introduction of the new system will not adversely affect other live systems; this is particularly important in an ERP solution where the HR/payroll or CRM solution may share a platform with other modules (for example, finance) which are already live.

TRAINING PREPARATION

As the test phase nears conclusion, preparation for training should also be almost complete, with the following tasks accomplished:

- training content finalized;

- training data generated;

- training environment ready to receive the UAT-d version of each system;

- data cleardown facilities available on the training system so that each set of delegates can start their training course with the data in the required state;

- training facilities ready;

- training courses scheduled and joining instructions issued.

OTHER TASKS

Other tasks that need to have been progressed during the test phase are:

- business readiness and communications planning on track;

- cutover preparation nearing finalization;

- data capture well advanced;

- capture and indexing of KM content complete;

- users allocated to roles;

- agreements reached on arrangements, operating level agreements (OLAs) with the supplier and the IT department for system support post-go-live.

GETTING SIGN-OFF TO THE TEST PHASE

The project manager should present a report to the project board that includes the UAT summary, describes progress against plan on the other tasks listed above, and updates project performance against the PID and business case. If the project board is satisfied that the test phase has been concluded satisfactorily, it will then grant authorization for the final preparation/cutover phase to commence.

Rollout Phase

Ahead of the deployment of any new HR systems users must first be trained. Training courses will use the specially created training data running on the latest version of the new system, preferably the one that has been UAT-approved. Sometimes, however, overall project deadlines do not allow this, in which case formal change control is vital to ensure that decisions are taken daily as to which fixes are applied to the training environment and when.

Like the UAT, the training will be process based, and hence will include system and non-system components to ensure that agents and other users are trained in the end-to-end business processes and not just in the use of the technology.

Trainees may be assessed at the end of each module and will complete training course evaluation sheets, so that the effectiveness of the training can be monitored. After training they may be given access to a 'sandpit' version of the system where they can gain further familiarization with the systems at their own pace.

CUTOVER PREPARATION

In tandem with training delivery, other tasks in preparation for cutover should be carried out, as described below.

Rehearsals

Depending on the system involved, and the extent and complexity of data conversion, it may be necessary to conduct one or more dry runs of cutover, in order to demonstrate that it can be accomplished safely and in a timely manner.

Support

Plans and SLAs should by now be in place with the supplier and in-house IT to provide post-go-live support; for example help desk, supplier telephone support and so on. Additional resources should also have been arranged for the 'storm period' (the weeks immediately following cutover), in order to ensure that any post-cutover spike in system-related incidents can be absorbed without disruption to service. Further storm period support may include:

- additional representatives of the supplier, who may need to be physically on site;

- representatives of the implementation partner;

- central and local in-house IT resources;

- project team members (for example, business analysts).

To take a more proactive stance, some of the team may be required to act as 'floorwalkers' in order to help identify any potential issues before they develop into major incidents.

Business Change and Implementation

The project should by now be approaching the final and most intense phase of executing its business change plan. A variety of briefings and communications with customer representatives in the business should have taken place over the previous months, and final plans should now be in place to ensure that cutover is managed as smoothly as possible from the customer's standpoint. For example, any specific cutover procedures or interim arrangements may need to be communicated to managers and employees at this point.

Live Environment Ready

The final (that is, post-UAT) version of the software should now be loaded onto the 'production' environment by the IT specialists, so that it is ready for live use.

Local PCs

Local PCs and printers should be readied for live operation, with user access and passwords in place, to be unlocked upon cutover.

Data Capture

Any data capture, for example email addresses, should be complete, with any necessary interim procedures in place to keep them up to date ahead of go-live.

Interfaces

Any initial interface runs (for example, updating the CRM with personal details of staff from the HR/payroll system) should be scheduled to run immediately prior to cutover.

Interim Procedures

Any interim procedures should be ready to be implemented; for example in a payroll system dealing with staff who are due back pay during the first live month may be unable to calculate this automatically because key historical data may not have been brought across from the legacy system.

'Go/No-Go' Decision

When final preparation is complete, the project manager should provide a report to the project board on training delivery and cutover preparation. This report should list the go/no-go criteria for the cutover decision, together with an assessment of the degree to which each has been satisfied, to give an at-a-glance view of cutover readiness, and highlight any outstanding issues. When the project board is satisfied that everything is in place, they will sign off the final preparation activity as complete, and authorize the commencement of cutover to live running of the service and supporting systems (see Appendix A for sample Go/No Go criteria).

As previously discussed, in a wider programme, for example HR transformation, the technology component may form merely one (albeit possibly the most complex) of a number of workstreams that will need to have successfully concluded their final preparation. In that case, responsibility for ensuring that all workstreams are ready for sign-off, and gaining a 'go' decision, rests with programme management.

Cutover and Stabilization

CUTOVER

Cutover tasks are likely to include:

- Conversion programs are run against appropriate live systems so that they are populated with data. In the case of a new HR/payroll system this will represent several days' work and may need to have been rehearsed previously. When the data have been converted they will need to be reconciled to ensure that they have migrated across correctly.

- Other critical data may need to be entered manually on the live system before normal operation can commence.

- User access profiles are unlocked so that users can access their systems.

- On the morning of go-live, the storm level support teams come in early and are ready to assist.

- The users come in early and receive any final briefing.

- The HR function gets to work and the users start to use the new system.

With these steps cutover has been concluded and the solution is now live.

Catch-up

Depending on the system, there may be an initial task to catch up with regular transactions that have been held back pending go-live.

STABILIZATION

Typically, when new systems are launched, the first few hours or days are relatively quiet, unless there is a major problem such as a system crash. Gradually, as users make time to try out the new system, transaction volumes increase and plateau at normal levels.

Incidents are logged as they arise and are investigated, and special attention needs to be given to more complex features such as some of the interfaces. Hopefully, however, the support teams, bolstered by the additional storm period resources, are able to resolve incidents and issues without undue service disruption, and the systems settle into their regular usage patterns.

The systems may need to be taken out of service at off-peak times during this initial period to allow groups of fixes to be released into them, following resolution of faults. Attention will also need to be paid to features that come on stream slightly later than cutover, for example the less regular MI reports that must await the aggregation of a week's or a month's worth of data before they can be run.

System performance needs to be kept under constant review until a decision can eventually be taken by operational management that support can be cut back to normal levels. This will signal the end of the storm period and mark the departure of the project team from the operational site. At this point the formalities of project closure can be addressed.

Project Closure

In order to close a project or programme, the following tasks are necessary:

- a list of all outstanding actions and issues should be prepared recommending how they should be addressed;

- all system documentation should be confirmed as having been completed and made available to relevant support teams and users;

- all project/programme documentation that is not relevant to supporting the live operation should be confirmed as having been completed, and then archived;

- a post-implementation review should be prepared by the project or programme manager, which:

    - assesses overall project performance against the business case and PID;

    - highlights any lessons learned;

    - lists outstanding tasks showing how and by whom they will be actioned; this should be presented to the project board, following which key points and outstanding actions should be referred to appropriate parties for resolution (see Appendix A for an example of post implementation review contents and approach);

- all project/programme accommodation, facilities and hardware should be returned their permanent owners;

- the project board and project team should be disbanded.

With these tasks accomplished, the project is complete and the new system is now under operational control.

SUMMARY OF CHAPTER MESSAGES

- Delivery is a complex and often lengthy process that needs to be managed carefully, using a variety of techniques; for example, risk and issue management and change control.

- Customization of the chosen product should be avoided. It is better to adapt business processes in line with the package, which should have been developed in line with best HR practice.

- The design of the solution should be determined by a series of workshops at which users' needs are translated by business analysts into documents that configurers can use when building the system. These documents should be signed off by the users.

- Appropriate approaches to system build should be deployed. For example, configuration allows additional opportunities for users to confirm that the system is being built in line with their expectations.

- A thorough system test should be carried out in order to ensure that the integrated solution works as specified.

- Following sign-off to the system test, an equally thorough user acceptance test (UAT) should be undertaken to ensure that the technology successfully supports the end-to-end business processes. In a payroll project, due regard should be given to parallel runs.

- Following sign-off to the UAT, system training should be delivered using a copy of the UAT-approved software and specially created training data that can be rolled back to its starting state for each new course.

- A business change and implementation workstream should run throughout the duration of system delivery, to ensure that customers are fully prepared for the changes that the technology will bring, and know how to make best use of its features.

- The project must ensure that all other implementation tasks (for example, data capture, data cleanse, hardware availability, cutover planning and so on) are also kept on track. Following completion of user training, the status of all project workstreams should be assessed in order to reach a decision on whether cutover from the old to the new system(s) should commence.

- The project should ensure that additional support resources are available for the 'storm period' following cutover. When the system is judged to have stabilized (that is, incidents and issues have reduced to expected steady state volumes), support should be scaled back to normal levels.

- Prior to project closure, a post implementation review should be carried out, and any outstanding actions and lessons learned from the project should be directed to appropriate operational management for attention.

PART IV

Building on Experience

Lessons Learned

So after 40 years of development and a wide range of projects of varying levels of success, what are the principal lessons that the HR practitioner can take from the experts in delivery of HR applications? In this final section we will explore some of the lessons from the collective experience of the HR managers, programme managers and end users who were interviewed as part of the research for to this book.

Service-led Design

The impetus for many HR technology projects is to support delivery of the Ulrich model within HR operations. The main driver for such a change is generally related to the delivery of improved service levels at lower cost to the business; however, the disproportionate cost of the technology component can lead to a 'technically led solution', where solution delivery eclipses the true business motives of the programme.

A critical objective at the outset of an HR transformation technology project is the need to establish how the solution will integrate with the overall design of the HR function and, hence, to ensure an appropriate level of business focus on the technical project. The HR technology solution will need to be clear from the outset how it will serve the needs of the shared service centre, the HR business partner, the centres of expertise, the line managers and the employees in the organization.

The service ethos should reflect in the service architecture for HR, particularly in the design of the MI strategy, the channel strategy for the service centre and the approach to knowledge management. Above all, technology is a tool for delivering business change – it is not an end in itself.

Focus on the Business Case

The historical development of HR systems reflects the HR objectives that were prevalent at the time but which are not reflected in the new model for HR. Thus, for most organizations, legacy solutions will not drive an HR transformation agenda, by virtue of their lack of functionality and lack of integration with the needs of customers, other back office applications and the business as a whole.

At the same time, the benefits offered by the transformation are defined in terms of service improvement and cost reduction and should be clearly articulated in the business case. If organizations fail to do this they will struggle to get past the large IT investment required to support the transition.

Clearly, a lack of investment in technology in the long term will result in systems that become a constraint on organizational development. For many organizations this can be such a problem that it becomes significantly easier to consider radical options of outsourcing HR processes together with supporting systems as a means of avoiding the capital investment required for the internal development of systems.

Thus, the onus will be on the HR transformation programme manager to demonstrate the value of HR technology and its direct linkage with the objectives of the change; in short, the programme manager must develop an early grasp of the business case for investment in new systems and present this as part of the early planning for new solutions.

Use Technology Intelligently

In any major HR change project, it is unlikely that technology expenditure may account for 70 to 80 per cent of the overall budget for change. With such disproportionate spend it is easy for a transformation project to become technically focused and defined by technology deliverables and milestones such as testing, data conversion and technical integration rather than delivery of business benefits.

Our research shows that large-scale ERP implementations typically deploy less than 25 per cent of the technology's available functionality. If nothing else, this would appear to vindicate the suggestion that there is a disconnect between what most technology projects provide and the reality of how the service will be delivered.

The onus is on the programme manager to ensure that the programme maintains a proper perspective on the role of technology and the business objectives it is serving. It is their job to ensure that the business requirement is fully articulated (as opposed to merely written down) and understood before attempting to apply technical solutions.

Technology design and roll out should always make reference to the fundamentals of the project charter, specifically:

- How does this contribute to the business case?

- How does it improve service levels in HR?

- How does it reduce costs?

Participate in the Design Process

Whilst this may sound an obvious point to some, it is surprising how many projects delegate the design and development process to a third party, citing the need to 'rely on the experts' to guide them in the design of systems. Whilst external expertise has a role in a systems delivery project, there is no excuse for being kept in the dark about critical design decisions that will affect the way in which the application is used in HR.

Any design process should place key users and stakeholders at the heart of the activity through carefully managed design workshops that deal with each process in HR in a detailed walkthrough with direct reference to the system. It is critical that users and stakeholders understand what they will be getting and the implications for HR process; it is not sufficient to obtain a user's signature on the bottom of a dense design document as evidence of 'sign off'.

The best designers will be able to articulate the planned design clearly and in a way that 'brings the system to life' for those who may be unfamiliar with what it can do. Detailed demonstrations, structured walk-throughs, proof of concept models and rigorous cross examination of the design team are an essential part of the process.

Integration is King

Once upon a time, HR systems were the preserve of the HR function, with interfaces to other systems defined by the boundaries of the HR organization. However, the new HR model extends demands for people data outside the boundaries of the HR function and creates the need for integration of HR data and process on a wide variety of levels:

- within critical integrated functions in HR, such as performance management, reward and development;

- between the contact centre and the functional HR experts in shared services;

- for producing cross-functional management information spanning HR, finance, production and procurement data.

Whilst the main players in the HR technology market have played out a 'functional arms race' to develop progressively more sophisticated applications, insufficient attention has been paid to the need for the integration of critical data across applications. For the practitioner selecting HR applications, attention to integration issues will pay far greater dividends than selection of solutions with a high level of advanced functionality.

Project Team Capability, not Software Selection, has the Biggest Impact on Success

Selecting the right solution is important to the success of the project, but it is not the most critical factor. Many software providers can point to organizations that have implemented first-class applications in an appalling manner and failed to achieve any real benefit. Similarly there are many examples of low-cost solutions that have been implemented intelligently and which deliver real strategic value to the organization. The difference is, in most cases, the capability of the delivery team and, in particular, the programme manager.

However, whilst they may place an intensive focus on software selection, many organizations neglect to spend anything like the same effort selecting someone with the appropriate skills to lead the project, in some instances even allocating this role solely on the basis of availability to do the job. Quite aside from the fact that the best person for the job is probably, by definition, the least available, this neglects the need to assess critical skills and strategies to ensure the delivery is low cost, low risk and robustly managed.

Manage the Transition, not just the Technology

Separation of the delivery of the technology from the drivers for the transformation is a recipe for disaster. It is critical that the focus of programme management is on the whole delivery programme. Successful transformation programmes are characterized by a number of key criteria:

- engagement with stakeholders early to design a service that the business actually needs rather than one that is defined by the parameters of the technology solution;

- development of an integrated 'one HR' model that ensures the primary relationships within HR work are fully integrated in terms of common process, knowledge sharing, service identity and shared values and purpose;

- expecting and acknowledging that resistance to the change is likely; tackling business resistance by building on early commitments, focusing on the basics that will make a visible early impact and managing expectations;

- establishment of post-implementation disciplines in HR to ensure a commercial approach to service management, customer focus, monitoring and management of service performance and financial accounting.

Practise Good Project Disciplines and Governance

Project management and delivery is a major topic in its own right and the secret of successful HR technology is, to large extent, synonymous with good project disciplines. Whilst these are too numerous to list here, particular issues for the HR programme manager to consider include:

- ensuring the critical project roles are in place, including appropriate project governance and direction, senior level sponsorship and clearly defined project team roles and structures;

- making intelligent use of project methodologies to ensure project delivery is properly structured without a slavish adherence to checklists and paperwork;

- ensuring critical project deliverables are clearly set out and communicated; key documentation includes a current state assessment, clearly defined scope and vision for the project, the business case for change, the project initiation document and the operational model for HR.

Configuration, not Customization

Most, if not all, of the HR transformation technology solution will be based on package technology from mainstream solution suppliers. Programme managers should understand that the true value of package technology comes from the embedded business processes they contain. These represent the collective experience of the programme developers as well as all existing users who have contributed their experience to the overall design of the solution.

Against this background it makes absolute sense that the supplied process is the starting point for any design decisions. Customizing the standard application is to be discouraged due to the risk, cost and support problems it creates, and the organization is well advised to change the process in preference to changing the system. More importantly, if the organization discovers that it cannot deliver a 'standard' HR process using supplied functionality from a mainstream supplier then it may be a good indication that this process needs to be rethought.

Act as an Intelligent Customer

An HR transformation technology project represents a major investment and a massive undertaking involving large numbers of internal resources and the deployment of external expertise around key technical and change-related roles.

It is easy to become overwhelmed in the face of so many expensively suited consultants and defer to the greater knowledge that they bring. However, it can be a fatal error to place too much faith in the capabilities of your external advisers. It is in the nature of the consulting business that consultants will seldom admit publicly to being out of their depth and certainly not to the client!

At the same time, there is a wealth of previous experience available from external sources and the programme manager should seize the opportunity to learn from what others have done, understand how they benchmark against other organizations and seek expert opinions as to 'what will work here'.

The key here is to act as an 'intelligent customer', developing an active relationship with advisers, bearing several key characteristics:

- asking intelligent, searching questions of your advisers to ensure due diligence; seeking the views of consultants on the relevant issues and how they apply here, asking where they have encountered similar situations before and assessing their capability to tackle issues that present themselves;

- insisting on good programme governance with effective project controls to identify problems early in the process;

- taking an honest and direct approach to confronting performance issues on the team, wherever they lie;

- understanding that no-one knows your organization better than your own people and keeping control of key decisions around design and delivery;

- at the same time, understanding the value of partnership and how to make it work effectively: success achieved by the consultant team will reflect well on them, the project and ultimately, you; beating up on your consultants for every mistake or shifting blame for problems does not reflect well on anyone; programme managers should develop an instinct for the things that are truly important and insist on them.

Conclusion

The history of HR systems has unrolled over four decades with much of that time spent establishing the functionality of the systems and the technical integration required to make them work effectively in an HR environment. Now, at the end of this period there is a wealth of systems available to the HR practitioner to support the agenda for change in HR. Whilst the issues in delivering such solutions are complex, the rewards are high in terms of the potential for significant improvements in service levels and significant reductions in operating costs.

At the same time, the fundamental shift in the organization and delivery of HR services initiated by David Ulrich and others means that technology change now routinely happens in the context of a wider transformational agenda and that success in delivering systems is dependent on a clear understanding of where technology can support the change (and where it cannot).

In the course of this book we have endeavoured to provide a guide for practitioners that steers a course through the complexities of systems delivery to achieve real and lasting benefits from technology solutions. We hope we have been successful and that this book will become a valuable reference for the journey.

It remains our firm belief that, whilst the technology may have become more complex over the years, the recipe for success for the programme manager lies firmly in non-technical areas. In particular, the HR transformation programme manager must possess the ability to take a commercial, business-focused view of the HR function and how it can be improved; sell that concept to the business and recognize that, whilst technology can be invaluable, it is, in the end, merely a tool.

Case Studies

How the NHS tackled scale and complexity to deliver HR systems for 1.3 million employees

BUSINESS CONTEXT

There can be few organizations globally that deal with the scale of HR management faced by the NHS, with over 1.3 million employees managed across a wide range of business units.

By 2000, the legacy systems for managing and paying the employees were coming to the end of their useful life. Sixty-five per cent of the employee base was paid via dated 'green screen' payroll technology that provided little or no pre-calculation functionality and required a high degree of manual effort to support.

At the same time, a focus on HR and payroll services revealed a significant opportunity to reduce headcount in favour of front-line services through centralization of transactional activity, single data entry and the development of integrated HR and payroll solutions.

SOLUTION SCOPE

Organizationally, the scope of the solution covered all staff with NHS employment contracts, including NHS trusts, in England and Wales as well as primary care staff, a total of 1.3 million employees. The solution excluded all private sector employees working in the NHS and GPs and their staff.

Functionally, the requirements covered a comprehensive range of applications including:

- core HR transactions and employee record keeping;
- payroll;

- recruitment;

- learning management systems (LMS);

- talent management;

- manager and employee self-service;

- inter-authority staff transfers;

- data warehouse.

DELIVERING THE PROGRAMME

Leading the initiative as programme manager for the NHS employee staff record (ESR) programme was Jim O'Connell.

'By 2001 we had narrowed the software choice to the two largest ERP providers, SAP and Oracle', said O'Connell. *'We were confident that either solution had the functional capabilities to do the job but overall felt that Oracle had a better focus on our business imperatives and had a more realistic, better paced, implementation approach.'*

The NHS finally chose a consortium approach comprising software solutions from Oracle and implementation services from both PWC and healthcare specialists McKesson.

O'Connell admits that the scale of the development very quickly brought the project into difficulties. An initial plan in early 2002 to deliver a pilot implementation across 40 NHS trusts within 12 months was rapidly extended by four months to April 2003. As the revised deadline approached it was apparent that this too was not likely to be achieved.

'In hindsight', O'Connell continues, *'we had poor understanding of the fitness for purpose of the out of the box technology, poor understanding of how much customization would be required and poor understanding of how we were going to implement on such a large scale. We placed too much trust in the "experts" and failed to recognise that some of them were clearly out of their depth.'*

After a publicly embarrassing failure to deliver a working pilot by the end of 2003, the programme was restructured and saw a senior programme manager from McKesson step up to take the solution delivery role alongside O'Connell and his team.

The team quickly moved to focus the project on delivering a working solution, and once this was achieved to ensure adequate take up by the NHS HR community. The organizations in which the solution would be deployed were autonomous trusts, legal entities in their own right, with no obligation to use the solution developed by O'Connell and his team. In addition, trusts' autonomy and independence from central control were increasing with the introduction of foundation trusts. Indeed, many had invested in their own solutions and were highly reluctant to accept a centrally driven solution.

Faced with a need to develop 'levers' to persuade all parts of the NHS to use the solution, the team took the decision to pay for the solution centrally so that the trusts would, in effect, get it for free. This made business cases for investment in local HR systems difficult to sustain in the face of a promise to deliver ESR at no charge and, hence, the trusts started to come into line.

The second hurdle was the delicate balance of the business case and the demands that it placed on the project. The return on investment identified by the business case was only achievable if the project delivered roll-out within two years. Given the early delays in the project there was very little contingency and it was critical that the tight timetable for roll-out of the solution was adhered to.

To address this, the project developed a rigorous approach to the roll-out plan. Each trust was expected to stick to a rigid timetable for the roll-out process and fines were imposed in the form of top-sliced budgets for those trusts that did not meet delivery timescales.

To ensure each area remained on track during the roll out period the team demanded achievement of defined goals at fixed periods:

- -14 to -11 months before the go-live date: any local requirements fully defined and documented;

- -11 to -8 months before go-live: project initiation document (PID), governance and sponsor in place;

- -8 months until go-live: a series of four readiness assessments were carried out, each of which would result in a 'go/no-go' decision for the project.

At the time of writing, the programme has been delivered to over 800,000 NHS employees in over 400 NHS trusts and is continuing with a roll-out programme that will go live in 'waves' of 100,000 employees every two months until completion in April 2008.

BENEFITS DELIVERED

Full delivery of benefits will be dependent on completion of the roll-out. However, the programme is on track to deliver the full financial benefits planned at the outset; specifically these include:

- a saving of approximately 900 FTEs as a result of integrating HR and payroll data entry;

- procurement savings arising from the development of a single HR system, thus avoiding multiple procurement projects across the organization to purchase and develop many local solutions; these savings were similarly estimated at £18m.

However, some of the most significant benefits arose from the development of a 'single version of the truth' for HR where previously had existed a multiplicity of fragmented databases. The end solution has allowed for a significant improvement in the quality and the scope of management information that HR is able to provide.

Significantly the solution provides a national data warehouse on NHS employment. For the first time this provides a repository of people data on an intra-authority basis that supports production of meaningful management information. In particular, it has allowed for a rapid collation of data for the annual medical and dental census which had previously been a major administrative task for an army of staff right across the NHS.

Lastly, the early focus on business critical issues such as absence management meant that, for the first time, the organization was able to monitor, benchmark and target absence and plan proactive policies for addressing the underlying causes.

WHAT NEXT?

Whilst the programme has still to complete the initial roll-out, this is now regarded as being relatively stable and O'Connell and the team have turned their attention to the next stage of developments.

'The initial roll-out was focused on the base applications, specifically core HR, payroll and recruitment as these areas carried the greatest weight of the business case.

Next on the agenda will be the delivery of self-service tools to both line managers and employees and learning and talent management functionality. Then we will look at areas where we can make more intelligent use of the system such as eLearning, access routes to clinical information systems and the development of executive dashboards.'

In addition, the delivery of a stable, common platform for HR data has now opened up the opportunity to develop full-scale shared services for the NHS. Although CRM is out of scope of the current delivery, it is expected to play an active part in the development of a shared services solution.

LESSONS LEARNED

Asked for his views on the lessons learned from the project, O'Connell responds quickly as though these have been deeply ingrained. He summarizes his observations and recommendations to others in similar situations in six main points:

- *Act as an intelligent customer*: Whilst the use of external experts is essential, so too is the need to ask informed questions and perform due diligence. Do not just assume that the experts know what they are doing. Important areas to test thoroughly and regularly include the capabilities of the team, the project disciplines they are using to drive the project and the estimating assumptions they are using.

- *Participate in the design*: This issue goes hand in hand with the first point and O'Connell traces many of the early problems of the programme to having been 'in the dark' when many critical design decisions were taken.

- *Change the process, not the system*: Learn from the capabilities of the new functionality and take advantage of what is offered in the new system. Projects should seize the opportunity to move away from legacy-driven methods. The NHS radically revised the payroll reconciliation process and adopted new methods as a result of reviewing the capabilities offered by the Oracle solution.

- *Don't underestimate the importance of the change process*: The best-designed systems will be valueless if they are not adopted by the organization. O'Connell points to the process of 'selling the solution' within the NHS as well as the rigorous assessment of readiness to proceed at each stage as being key indicators of success.

- *Understand the meaning of partnership*: Major programmes rely on partnerships with a range of internal and external resources.

Problems experienced by your partners will reflect badly on the programme and, ultimately, on you. True partnership means being accountable for the successes of your partners; in other words, making your partners look good. Working with partners does not mean ignoring problems, nor does it mean beating up on every mistake. Instead, programme managers should develop an instinct for the things that are really important to ask for.

- *Develop local ownership of the solution*: Programme managers running large corporate projects run the risk of isolation from the business. Develop an understanding of the issues faced by the users 'at the coal face' and adopt the language of the users as a means of building rapport and ownership of the delivered solution.

How technology has enabled Norwich Union to develop and broaden HR delivery?

THE BUSINESS CONTEXT

Norwich Union Insurance (NUI) is part of the Aviva Group, formed by an aggressive merger and acquisition strategy during the late 1990s, culminating firstly in the merger of General Accident with Commercial Union and then with Norwich Union during 2000. The Aviva group is the largest insurer in the UK, employing 34,000 staff and around 58,000 staff globally, operating within an industry subjected to very tight regulatory compliance overseen by the Financial Services Authority (FSA) .

As with all mergers and acquisitions, HR found themselves under immediate pressure to re-align the newly formed business into a single organization, resulting in intense restructuring activity, organization design, selection and appointment, relocation of staff, redeployment, redundancy as well as driving out operational inefficiencies through standardization, removal of duplication, process re-engineering and so on. HR not only had to demonstrate that it could become more efficient and cost effective, but most importantly, support the business with strategic business change.

HR functions were organized conventionally but decentralized across the group, although Norwich Union itself had implemented a shared service model in 1999. In 2003 a shared service model was acknowledged as the best way forward and adopted as a strategy cornerstone going forward.

The legacy of business mergers and acquisition had resulted in a multiplicity of inherited HR systems that were relied on to produce immediate and accurate management information to support 'business as usual' and future organizational changes. At the same time, HR was required to review and recommend the best technology to transform HR to deliver cost-effective processes.

KEY DRIVERS FOR HR

HR had inherited a variety of payroll and administration systems, since the business had grown a number of local databases designed to support local initiatives, as central data did not have the credibility to be relied on.

A typical example was the existence of a variety of training administration systems – databases holding details of mandatory training subject to FSA scrutiny. The information held centrally did not capture contingent workers and therefore resulted in a mismatch of data between central and decentralized systems.

At this point it would have been easy to simply review products, in this context narrowing choice down to Tier 1 solutions offered by Oracle, SAP and PeopleSoft powerful enough to handle what NUI described themselves as simply a 'workhorse solution'. However, they chose to adopt a number of strategic design principles to help inform their choice:

- The new technology platform had to be able to run the existing and future HR organization, particularly a shared services delivery model;

- The product had to offer strong integration capability;

- Product flexibility was key, offering maximum configuration capability to enable minimal customization;

- It must be scalable and at the same time offer cost-effective ownership to the business;

- It had to achieve a single source of employee data for the entire UK-wide group.

At the same time, there was clearly a longer term vision for HR aimed at exploiting further value from its shared service operation through the deployment of new technology in order to deliver more self-service transactions, enhance access to employee information for staff and line managers and broaden access to a wider range of HR services. Underpinning this approach were plans to web-enable as many routine transactions as possible and maximize the use of workflow in order to reduce workload throughout the organization, not just in HR.

THE SOLUTION

Following a competitive process, Oracle HR and payroll was chosen as the UK-wide solution (in fact Oracle payroll had already been implemented a couple of years earlier in Norwich Union so they had already gained considerable knowledge of the product) and was implemented in 2001, decommissioning all other systems. Delivering the common platform enabled HR to move to a single shared service operation in 2003, simultaneously commencing the roll-out of self-service phased over 18 months. Significantly, the positive acceptance of on-line payslips demonstrated a clear message to HR that, if delivered properly, web-enabled HR would be readily adopted by staff.

In 2005, Aviva acquired the RAC, an organization with a very different range of T&Cs, working practices and job types. The challenge of course was to swiftly migrate onto the Oracle platform with minimum disruption, a task completed successfully following some complex T&C negotiations, leaving the way for the decommissioning of the legacy payroll system.

Successful implementation and consolidation of the new HR and payroll platform, in particular delivering the single source of employee data goal that HR had demanded, provided sufficient evidence to secure further investment funding in their technology transformation strategy. The integrated nature of the technical solution has enabled HR to develop a growing range of services exploiting the modular nature of the Oracle product:

- *contingent worker*: allowing active management of agency/contract workers through the system;

- *compensation workbench*: allowing line managers to undertake on-line salary reviews and modelling;

- *i-surveys*: in development and key to UK-wide employee engagement assessment;

- *call logging*: supporting the shared service contact centre;

- *LMS and i-recruitment*: both in the process of implementation.

BENEFIT DELIVERY

Norwich Union's ongoing commitment to Oracle HR technology is sufficient evidence in itself of the substantial benefit they believe it has delivered, particularly when it is considered to be such an integral feature of HR's shared service operation. Indeed, establishing benefit attributable to technology alone is not possible given the inclusive way they view the relationship between business model, process and technology.

Having said that it is possible to establish the benefit of some specific technology initiatives, for example saving £60,000 per annum in print and distribution costs following implementation of on-line payslips and £240,000 per annum in reduced staff costs due to the elimination of double keying in HR administration when Oracle self-service was implemented. In parallel, a previous process of tracking the continuous improvement of HR performance against SLAs was eliminated as the database was updated immediately by the manager or staff member.

Norwich Union now has the ability to obtain the true costs of IT support and development for HR IT and of course the very real benefit to the whole organization of having confidence in a single source of accurate employee data.

What is clear is that Norwich Union has been able to successfully blend good organizational design with the selection of the right technology to create a very effective delivery model which keeps pace with the needs of the organization, staff and the HR function itself.

How Fujitsu Telecoms replaced an underperforming payroll system with a solution that complemented IT as well as HR strategy

THE BUSINESS CONTEXT

Fujitsu Telecoms is a wholly owned subsidiary of its Japanese parent and is recognized as a market leader in the provision of telecommunications products and services with an annual turnover of around £220 million. In the UK Fujitsu employs 800 staff plus a large contingent workforce, driven by the fluctuating demands of the market, of which around 120 graduate engineers work in product development with the remainder working mainly in a civil engineering capacity in an installation and infrastructure division.

A lean HR function of eight staff in total support the business, operating with business partners/advisers and a small central team. Payroll responsibility is held by Fujitsu's finance function.

In the run-up to 'year 2000' Fujitsu discovered that their existing payroll system was not compliant and, fearing that the system could possibly 'fall over', hurriedly selected a replacement HR and payroll system. Implementation was undertaken by a partner who demonstrated poor understanding of their process and operating model, resulting in a rapid but unsatisfactory implementation compounded by poor training of Fujitsu's own staff.

Over the next few years much of HR's priority was focused upon supporting the business through major restructuring, but it became all too apparent that the hasty implementation was creating serious technical and functional performance problems to such an extent that falling service quality was considered a risk to the business. HR's ability to deal with this was compromised through having little or no internal capability to tackle the problem, which by 2004 became critical when they were advised that the product would no longer be supported by the vendor. The choice was stark: either upgrade to a new version or consider alternative solutions.

KEY DRIVERS FOR HR

HR change strategy in Fujitsu is constructed around a low cost of delivery model managed through a network of business partners/advisers working closely with the business. Self-service, integration of some key internal systems, such as time and attendance, and cost centre management, as well as rectifying a number of complex and expensive interfaces were considered key to moving the strategy forward. Any new system therefore had to be able to demonstrate breadth of functionality, high system integration capability and low cost of ownership.

HR were also acutely aware of the difficulties caused by having little internal support capability, relying on expensive external resources. At the same time they realized that Fujitsu itself had an established software development business line with Oracle and as a result possessed significant

internal Oracle capability. In terms of product selection this presented them
with a dilemma:

- business requirement could be met by a low-cost Tier 2 solution
  given the size and complexity of the business;

- preference was for a more expensive Tier 1 solution given internal
  Oracle expertise;

- budget was based upon a Tier 2 solution.

THE SOLUTION

In early 2005 Fujitsu embarked upon a product selection process including
both Tier 1 and 2 vendors, coinciding with a change of strategy at Oracle,
now anxious to compete on cost for Tier 2 business given the narrowing of the
'functionality gap' over recent years. Oracle were offering a product, 'Oracle
Simply', containing all of the fundamentals of HR, payroll and self-service on
the basis of an 'out of the box' implementation using a configuration tool in order
to minimize implementation and license costs as well as speed of delivery.

On this basis Oracle were selected, after adjusting the business case to
include the cost of business implementation resources since Oracle only
provide sufficient technical resource to implement the standard solution. The
project was to be split into two phases:

- phase 1 – payroll and time and attendance

- phase 2 – self-service

Fujitsu engaged Arinso as implementation partner and, together with
three internal HR resources in support, phase 1 implementation began in
July 2005, commencing with design workshops through test and parallel run
phases to full implementation in November 2005. Oracle's Discover reporting
tool is also used alongside a bespoke Fujitsu finance cost management
system.

BENEFIT DELIVERY

Fujitsu's HR Director believes that despite a small number of implementation
problems, the system is delivering business case benefits:

- a reduction of 20 per cent in HR headcount;

- cost of ownership reduced;

- technical objectives achieved, that is, internal resource capability and reduced complexity;

- scalable solution enabling further development of HR strategy;

- greater support to business partners/advisers through the provision of high quality MI, that is, management of absence and performance management processes.

How Lloyds TSB used technology to deliver a 'step change' in the further transformation of its HR shared service delivery model

THE BUSINESS CONTEXT

In 1997, just one year after the merger of Lloyds and TSB, the bank's HR division began implementation of the largest shared service in the financial services sector. This was the bank's first foray into shared services and was seen by the board as very much an experiment to determine whether the significant theoretical benefits attributable to the strategy could in fact be delivered, particularly in terms of cost reduction and service improvement.

PA Consulting worked with the in-house team to develop a long-term strategy, from initial concept pilot through to full business wide implementation and extending to business process outsourcing (BPO) opportunities, with review checkpoints at the end of each phase aimed at ensuring that further development would only be sanctioned if commercially viable.

Pilot and implementation phases were successfully delivered by 1999, coinciding with the completion of many of the most important post-merger plans (reorganization/removal of duplicated functions and activities and so on), at which point a company-wide efficiency programme was launched, aimed at delivering sustainable cost-reduction benefit for reinvestment in the business through a 'root and branch' organization and process reengineering drive.

KEY DRIVERS FOR HR

For HR this presented the opportunity to drive their strategy further forward. It was already apparent that shared service back-office cost savings had more or less plateaued at around 30 per cent of their base point given their heavy reliance on largely manually driven transactional processes.

An alarmingly rapid growth of and reliance on desktop systems, with all the associated risks and multiple versions of employee data needed to support business units with varying T&Cs and policies, was also giving cause for concern. Of particular concern were labour intensive and often fragmented processes governed by regulatory bodies where speed of 'on boarding' was deemed business critical yet at the same time subject to strict internal and external compliance scrutiny.

Further devolvement of HR accountabilities to line managers was not possible given the understandable refusal to take on additional activity without any obvious benefit and the growing amount of time business partners were spending resolving operational issues, negating the positive benefit of their strategic role.

So, from a shared service perspective, it was clear that the adoption of the best ERP technology would be essential if continued improvements in service delivery and cost reduction agendas were to be maintained.

But what of the existing HR system itself?

Post merger, TSB's HR and payroll system was migrated onto Lloyds existing HR and payroll platform. By 1999 customization levels were approaching 75 per cent, with the associated cost of maintenance and development and reliance on a small skilled resource pool. Lack of flexibility (to enable development of self-service in particular) was severely limiting HR's capability to change further. This problem was further exacerbated by an environment littered with a variety of legacy systems and over 100 interfaces.

It was also recognized that many core HR processes had been adapted rather than redesigned to fit the shared service model, adding complexity, lengthening end-to-end process time and raising both HR staffing and IT support/development costs. The business itself had also moved forward from simply having raised expectations of improved service from HR (given the success of the new model) to one of setting stretching annual service improvement targets.

THE SOLUTION

From a shortlist of just two, Oracle's core HR module with self-service was selected, with a plan to migrate all non-payroll functionality onto the new platform, leaving payroll processing on the exisitng system and at the same time outsourcing payroll 'gross to net' processing to Ceridian. Computer

Science Corporation (CSC) were selected, through a competitive process, as implementation partners to work as part of an integrated programme team not only because of their obvious technical and product capability but also their rapid application development methodology, which was considered complementary to LTSB's and essential given the need to achieve early benefit delivery. This phase of the programme was delivered in nine months.

Simultaneously, responsibility for many HR transactions was devolved to line management to announce the arrival of self-service, as well as eliminating paperwork and most importantly transferring decision-making accountability from HR to the line managers, by using the already well-established telephony channel ahead of implementing self-service on-line.

On-line self-service was delivered on a phased basis over the following twelve months to around 65,000 employees. Deployment of the self-service functionality itself was straightforward, with the biggest challenges focused on delivering single sign-on, dealing with variations in desktop PC build, building organizational hierarchies and change management support.

The CSC team remained in place for the first 12 months, before scaling down to a handful, at which time it was felt that sufficient knowledge had been acquired internally to deliver the remaining projects. Overall, from mobilization to completion, the project was completed in 24 months.

BENEFIT DELIVERY

Business case benefits delivered on this programme were significant. Headcount savings of over 200 in HR and 90 (as a result of improvements in self-service processes) across the business were achieved accompanied by annual cost savings of over £8 million. Return on investment was over 30 per cent. Deploying the product without customization and re-engineering over 50 core HR processes were the key factors but the project also delivered shortened process times, up to 80 per cent in some cases, and improved process quality, particularly around payroll transactions.

Technical complexity of the HR operating platform was significantly reduced along with IT support costs and, importantly, change request turnaround times.

Since implementation LTSB have taken a 'best of breed' approach, adding performance and learning management and flexible benefit systems to their shared service platform built upon the solid base provided by the core Oracle product.

Strategically, completion of the modernization of the technology base combined with a mature shared service and business partner culture has enabled LTSB to now move into the world of BPO with some confidence, and recently they completed a deal with Xansa covering the off-shoring of much of their back-office transaction processing and mass call-centre activities.

Glossary of Terms and Abbreviations

ACD	Automatic call distribution
BACS	Bankers automated clearing system
BP	Business partner (or business practices)
BPO	Business process outsourcing
CBT	Computer based training
CMS	Contact management system
CofE	Centre of expertise/excellence
CRM	Customer relationship management
CSC	Computer Science Corporation
CTI	Computer telephony Integration
eDRMS	Electronic document and records system
e-forms	Electronic forms (accessible via web based systems)
ERP	Enterprise resource planning
ESR	Employee staff records
ESS	Employee self service
FAQ	Frequently asked questions

FSA   Financial services authority

FTE   Full time equivalent

GL   General ledger

GP   General practioner

GTN   Gross to net

HR   Human resources

HR BP   Human resource business partner

HR SSC   Human resource shared service centre

HRIS   Human resource information system

HRM   Human resource management

HRTT   Human resource transformation technology

HTTP   Hypertext transfer protocol

ID&V   Indentification and verification

ILS   Integrated learning system

IT   Information technology

IVR   Interactive voice response

JAD   Joint application development

KM   Knowledge management

KPI   Key performance indicator

L&D   Learning and development

LAN   Local area network

LMS	Learning management system
MAT B1	Maternity leave certificate
MI	Management information
MIS	Management information system
MSS	Manager self service
NHS	National Health Service
NI	National insurance
O&M	Organisation and methods
OLA	Operating level agreement
OM	Organisation management
PBX	Private branch exchange
PC	Personal computer
PID	Project initiation document
PRINCE2	Projects in a controlled environment (PRINCE2 being the most recent version of this methodology)
QA	Quality assurance
RAD	Rapid application development
RAG status	Red, amber, green status
RICE	Reports, interfaces, conversion, enhancements
RMS	Recruitment (or Resourcing) management system
SAP	Systemanalyse und Programmentwicklung (One of the market leading ERP providers)

SLA   Service level agreement

SME   Subject matter expert

SOA   Service oriented architecture

SSC   Shared service centre

T&A   Time and attendance

T&Cs   Terms and conditions

TCP/IP   Transmission control protocol/Internet protocol

TPR   Test problem reporting

UAT   User acceptance testing

UAT   User acceptance testing

WAN   Wide area network

Appendix A:
Sample HR Technology Project Deliverables

Appendix 1: Sample contents list for a typical HR technology requirements document and request for proposal (RFP)

Table of Contents

Appendix 2: Example HR technology evaluation scoresheet and criteria

Implementation Process and Team

	Weight 1-10	Score 1-10	Total Score	Potential Maximum Score	% Score
Milestone plan well defined	5	4	20	50	40%
Timing of phasing	5	2	10	50	20%
Risk assessment and mitigation	5	4	20	50	40%
Appropriate use of implementation resources	5	1	5	50	10%
Experience of similar implementations in the sector	5	4	20	50	40%
Accreditation	5	6	30	50	60%
Evidence of appropriately skilled resource	5	6	30	50	60%
Availability of proposed team	5	2	10	50	20%
Quality Management	5	5	25	50	50%
Project Management	5	1	5	50	10%
Escalation process	5	5	25	50	50%
Transition approach	5	5	25	50	50%
Data migration	5	5	25	50	50%
Interfaces	5	5	25	50	50%
User training	5	8	40	50	80%
Customisation and configuration	5	6	30	50	60%
TOTAL	**80**	**69**	**345**	**800**	**43%**

Functional Fit

	Weight 1-10	Score 1-10	Total Score	Potential Maximum Score	% Score
HR functional fit					
Recruitment	5	2	10	50	20%
People In	5	5	25	50	50%
Changes	5	5	25	50	50%
Absence	5	5	25	50	50%
Reward	5	6	30	50	60%
Grievence and Discipline	5	5	25	50	50%
Learning and Development	5	4	20	50	40%
People Out	5	5	25	50	50%
Staff Allocation	5	0	0	50	0%
Payroll Functional Fit	5	6	30	50	60%
User Training fit	5	8	40	50	80%
Reporting fit	5	5	25	50	50%
Workflow, MSS & ESS fit	5	5	25	50	50%
Interfaces fit	5	5	25	50	50%
Data Integrity & Security fit	5	5	25	50	50%
TOTAL	**75**	**71**	**355**	**750**	**47%**

Technical & Architecture Fit

	Weight 1-10	Score 1-10	Total Score	Potential Maximum Score	% Score
Compliance with IT Architecture Standards	5	5	25	50	50%
Integration	5	5	25	50	50%
Scalability	5	6	30	50	60%
Backup & Recovery	5	7	35	50	70%
System & Data Integrity	5	4	20	50	40%
Privacy/Security	5	5	25	50	50%
Ease of Client Deployment	5	6	30	50	60%
Data Migration	5	7	35	50	70%
TOTAL	**40**	**45**	**225**	**400**	**56%**

Vendor

	Weight 1-100	Score 1-10	Total Score	Potential Maximum Score	% Score
Credibility and track record in HR and Payroll	5	8	40	50	80%
Understanding of Industry/Sector needs	5	6	30	50	60%
Customer base and track record in the UK	5	3	15	50	30%
Reference site relevence	5	0	0	50	0%
Reference site response and review	5	0	0	50	0%
Long term robustness of company	5	7	35	50	70%
TOTAL	**30**	**24**	**120**	**300**	**40%**

Appendix 3: Example high level project plan

Sample HR/Payroll Project Plan – High Level View

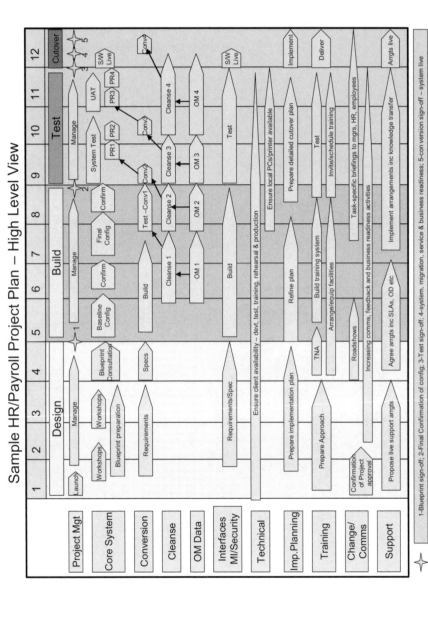

1-Blueprint sign-off; 2-Final Confirmation of config; 3-Test sign-off; 4-system, migration, service & business readiness; 5-con version sign-off – system live

Appendix 4: Risks and issues log

Sample Risk and Issues Log

Ref	Risk/Issue Name	Risk and Issues Statement	Risk/Issue Status	Impact (HML)	Probability (HML)	Mitigating actions	Who	When	Action Status
1	Hardware availability	Hardware may not be available within the required timescales due to long lead time needed for procurement. **Impact Description** This would delay Project critical path and hence Project go-live date	Open	H	M	1) Establish whether feasible to share existing hardware	Technology Workstream Lead	31/03/07	Open
						2) Pursue fast-track route for hardware procurement	Technology Workstream Lead	31/03/07	Open
2	Getting business decisions	Robust mechanism not yet in place for getting business decisions on key Project issues **Impact Assessment** This could result in late or inappropriate delivery	Open	H	L	1) Address formally via setting up appropriate govenance	Project Manager	15/03/07	Open
						2) Address informally by establishing hotline with Project Sponsor	Project Manager	01/03/07	Closed
3	Scope control	Initially scope appears containable, but this may be challenged during requirements or design workshops **Impact Assessment** Danger of exceeding budget and/or timescales	Open	H	L	1) Establish robust change control mechanism	Project Manager	15/03/07	Open
						2) Ensure Business signs off final scope	Project Manager	31/05/07	Open
4	Management Information subject matter expert	Management Information SME not yet allocated to Project **Impact Assessment** Design could be incomplete or incorrect	Open	M	L	1) Pursue formally to secure resource	Project Manager	15/03/07	Open
						2) Pending action 1, establish informal MI contact mechanism to get required input	Business Analyst	01/03/07	Closed

Appendix 5: Progress reporting

ORION

Progress Reporting

- The Progress Report will generally contain:

  - Name of project and Project Manager, date of report, Project stage and overall RAG status.
  - You may also give an overview of project – this should be a paragraph at most
  - Update on the cost summary – based on measure of resource used, costs spent etc
  - A list and an update on the key milestones (e.g agreed delivery date, whether started, in progress or completed, their individual RAG status, Forecast delivery date and actual delivery date)
  - A progress summary – what's been achieved over past x weeks, what's going to be achieved over next x weeks
  - Any issues and risks for escalation
  - Update on any dependencies
  - Anything else that is relevant

- A Progress Report gives an update on the project progress – and may be one of the communication tools you defined as part of the project communication.

- The report is owned by the project manager.

- The report needs to be issued regularly (as defined and agreed in the PID) to the agreed circulation.

- The RAG status (Red, Amber, Green) is used as an indication of progress and to highlight any concerns.

Appendix 6: Sample test progress summary

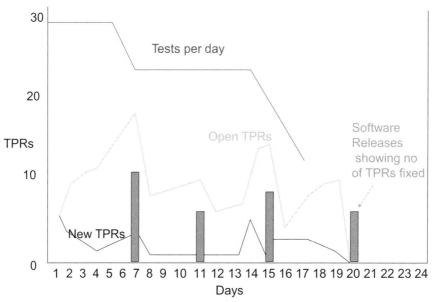

Sample Test Progress Summary

Appendix 7: Sample Go/No Go Criteria

Sample Go / No Go Criteria				
Readiness Type	**Criterion**	**Project Activity Manager**	**Sign-off**	**Date/ current RAG Status**
Solution Readiness	No high severity defects outstanding from testing	Solutions Workstream Lead	HR Director	23/09/07
Solution Readiness	Workrounds available for all other defects	Solutions Workstream Lead	HR Director	23/09/07
Solution Readiness	User documentation ready	Solutions Workstream Lead	HR Director	23/09/07
Solution Readiness	Payroll Parallel Run signed off	Solutions Workstream Lead	Payroll Manager	16/09/07
Data Readiness	Data conversion rehearsal signed off as satisfactory by Business	Business Change Workstream Lead	Business Implementation Manager	30/09/07
Technical Readiness	Cutover of software complete and confirmed	Technology Workstream Lead	Technology Director	30/09/07
Site Readiness	User site printers, PCs etc checked	Technology Workstream Lead	Business Implementation Manager	23/09/07
Operational Readiness	Live IT Support Team trained and ready to provide live support service	Solutions Workstream Lead	Technology Director	23/09/07
Operational Readiness	Live Business Support Team trained and ready to provide live support service	Business Change Workstream Lead	HR Director	30/09/07
Operational Readiness	Special Governance arrangements in place to manage transition and immediate post—live period	Project Manager	Project Board	23/09/07
Business Readiness	System training for all users completed satisfactorily	Business Change Workstream Lead	HR Director	30/09/07
Business Readiness	All user sites briefed and ready on new processes and procedures	Business Change Workstream Lead	HR Director	30/09/07

Appendix 8: Post implementation review

ORION

Post Implementation Review

- The Post Implementation Review will generally contain:
  - A list of key workstreams (e.g. training, communications, IT, Resourcing etc.)
  - A review of what went well and what could have been done differently for each workstream
  - A list of actions to take forward with owners and timescales

- After the Project Close, there also needs to be a **Benefits Review** to ascertain whether the benefits identified have been realised as part of the project delivery. This needs to be carried out at a suitable point after the project (usually 3-6 months after project delivery) and can be facilitated by the Project Manager or the Benefits owners.

- The purpose of this review is to review how the project worked, and to identify learning to be taken forward into future projects – both in terms of what went well (so do more off this) and what could be done differently (so consider doing differently next time)

- The project manager needs to keep a note (and should encourage project team members to do the same) during the duration of the project so that a full record of the project is kept.

- A post implementation review meeting needs to be held with the project team about 4 weeks after the project delivery. Much later than this, and the team have forgotten.

- The Benefits Review is a key project activity – and is often forgotten – as it ensures that a check is carried out to confirm whether the benefits identified have actually been realised by the project delivery.

Index

If you have found this book useful you may be interested in other titles from Gower

Addiction at Work:
Tackling Drug Use and Misuse in the Workplace
Edited by Hamid Ghodse
978-0-566-08619-9

Age Matters:
Employing, Motivating and Managing Older Employees
Keren Smedley and Helen Whitten
978-0-566-08680-9

The CEO: Chief Engagement Officer
Turning Hierarchy Upside Down to Drive Performance
John Smythe
978-0-566-08561-1

Handbook of Corporate University Development
Edited by Rob Paton, Geoff Peters, John Storey and Scott Taylor
978-0-566-08583-3

HR Business Partners
Ian Hunter, Jane Saunders, Allan Boroughs and Simon Constance
978-0-566-08625-0

HR Guide to Workplace Fraud and Criminal Behaviour
Michael J. Comer and Timothy E. Stephens
978-0-566-08555-0

Human Resources Outsourcing:
Solutions, Suppliers, Key Processes and the Current Market
Ian Hunter and Jane Saunders
978-0-566-08801-8

Practical Success Management:
How to Future-Proof Your Organization

Andrew Munro

978-0-566-08570-3

Senior Executive Reward:
Key Models and Practices

Sandy Pepper

978-0-566-08733-2

Requisite Organization:
A Total System for Effective Managerial Organization and
Managerial Leadership for the 21st Century

Elliott Jaques

978-0-566-07940-5

Strategic HR:
Building the Capability to Deliver

Peter Reilly and Tony Williams

978-0-566-08674-8

Systems Leadership:
Creating Positive Organizations

Ian Macdonald, Catherine Burke and Karl Stewart

978-0-566-08700-4

Vetting and Monitoring Employees:
A Guide for HR Practitioners

Gillian Howard

978-0-566-08613-7

For further information on these and all our titles visit our website –
www.gowerpub.com
All online orders receive a discount